Mussolini and Fascism: The View from America

Max Weber: Politics and the Spirit of Tragedy

The Problem of Authority in America

The Bard of Savagery: Thorstein Veblen

On Hallowed Ground:
Abraham Lincoln and the Foundations of American History

The Promise of Pragmatism:
Modernism and the Crisis of Knowledge and Authority

The Lost Soul of American Politics:
Virtue, Self-Interest, and the Foundations of Liberalism

The Proud Decades: America in War and in Peace, 1941–1960

Rise and Fall of the American Left

Up from Communism

The Liberal Persuasion

John Adams

John Patrick Diggins

John Adams

THE AMERICAN PRESIDENTS

ARTHUR M. SCHLESINGER, JR., GENERAL EDITOR

Times Books

HENRY HOLT AND COMPANY, NEW YORK

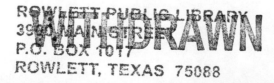

Times Books
Henry Holt and Company, LLC
Publishers since 1866
115 West 18th Street
New York, New York 10011

Henry Holt® is a registered trademark of Henry Holt and Company, LLC.

LIBRARY OF CONGRESS CATALOGING-IN-PUBLICATION DATA
Diggins, John P.
    John Adams / John Patrick Diggins.—1st ed.
        p. cm.—(The American presidents series)
    Includes bibliographical references and index.
    ISBN: 0-8050-6937-2
    1. Adams, John, 1735–1826. 2. Presidents—United States—Biography.
3. United States—Politics and government—1797–1801. I. Title.
II. American presidents series (Times Books (Firm))
E322.D54 2003
973.4'4'092—dc21
[B]   2002041392

Henry Holt books are available for special promotions and premiums.
For details contact: Director, Special Markets.

First Edition 2003

Printed in the United States of America
1 3 5 7 9 10 8 6 4 2

TO

PAUL BERMAN

Your letter touches my heart. Oh, that I may always be able to say to my grandsons, "You have learned much and behave well, my lads, Go on and improve in everything worthy."

Have you considered the meaning of that word "worthy"? Weigh it well. . . . I had rather you should be worthy possessors of one thousand pounds honestly acquired by your own labor and industry, than of ten millions by banks and tricks. I should rather you be worthy shoemakers than secretaries of states or treasury acquired by libels in newspapers. I had rather you be worthy makers of brooms and baskets than unworthy presidents of the United States procured by intrigue, factious slander and corruption.

—*John Adams to John Adams Smith, February 2, 1812*

The science of government is my duty. . . . I must study politics and war, that my sons may have liberty to study mathematics and philosophy. My sons ought to study mathematics and philosophy, geography and natural history and naval architecture, navigation, commerce, and agriculture, in order to give their children a right to study painting, poetry, music, architecture, statuary, tapestry, and porcelain.

—*John Adams to Abigail Adams, no date, 1790*

Under *Adams* as under *Jefferson* the government will sink. The party in the hands of whose chief it shall sink will sink with it and the advantage will all be on the side of his adversaries.

—*Alexander Hamilton to Theodore Sedgwick, May 19, 1800*

Contents

Editor's Note

THE AMERICAN PRESIDENCY

The president is the central player in the American political order. That would seem to contradict the intentions of the Founding Fathers. Remembering the horrid example of the British monarchy, they invented a separation of powers in order, as Justice Brandeis later put it, "to preclude the exercise of arbitrary power." Accordingly, they divided the government into three allegedly equal and coordinate branches—the executive, the legislative, and the judiciary.

But a system based on the tripartite separation of powers has an inherent tendency toward inertia and stalemate. One of the three branches must take the initiative if the system is to move. The executive branch alone is structurally capable of taking that initiative. The Founders must have sensed this when they accepted Alexander Hamilton's proposition in the Seventieth Federalist that "energy in the executive is a leading character in the definition of good government." They thus envisaged a strong president—but within an equally strong system of constitutional accountability. (The term *imperial presidency* arose in the 1970s to describe the situation when the balance between power and accountability is upset in favor of the executive.)

The American system of self-government thus comes to focus in the presidency—"the vital place of action in the system," as Woodrow Wilson put it. Henry Adams, himself the great-grandson and grandson of presidents as well as the most brilliant of American historians, said that the American president "resembles the commander of a ship at sea. He must have a helm to grasp, a course to steer, a port to seek." The men in the White House (thus far only men, alas) in steering their chosen courses have shaped our destiny as a nation.

Biography offers an easy education in American history, rendering the past more human, more vivid, more intimate, more accessible, more connected to ourselves. Biography reminds us that presidents are not supermen. They are human beings too, worrying about decisions, attending to wives and children, juggling balls in the air, and putting on their pants one leg at a time. Indeed, as Emerson contended, "There is properly no history; only biography."

Presidents serve us as inspirations, and they also serve us as warnings. They provide bad examples as well as good. The nation, the Supreme Court has said, has "no right to expect that it will always have wise and humane rulers, sincerely attached to the principles of the Constitution. Wicked men, ambitious of power, with hatred of liberty and contempt of law, may fill the place once occupied by Washington and Lincoln."

The men in the White House express the ideal and the values, the frailties and the flaws, of the voters who send them there. It is altogether natural that we should want to know more about the virtues and the vices of the fellows we have elected to govern us. As we know more about them, we will know more about ourselves. The French political philosopher Joseph de Maistre said, "Every nation has the government it deserves."

At the start of the twenty-first century, forty-two men have made it to the oval office. (George W. Bush is counted our forty-third president, because Grover Cleveland, who served nonconsecutive terms, is counted twice.) Of the parade of presidents, a dozen or so lead the polls periodically conducted by historians and political scientists. What makes a great president?

Great presidents possess, or are possessed by, a vision of an ideal America. Their passion, as they grasp the helm, is to set the ship of state on the right course toward the port they seek. Great presidents also have a deep psychic connection with the needs, anxieties, dreams of people. "I do not believe," said Wilson, "that any man can lead who does not act . . . under the impulse of a profound sympathy with those whom he leads—a sympathy which is insight—an insight which is of the heart rather than of the intellect."

"All of our great presidents," said Franklin D. Roosevelt, "were leaders of thought at a time when certain ideas in the life of the nation had to be clarified." So Washington incarnated the idea of federal union, Jefferson and Jackson the idea of democracy, Lincoln union and freedom, Cleveland rugged honesty. Theodore Roosevelt and Wilson, said FDR, were both "moral leaders, each in his own way and his own time, who used the presidency as a pulpit."

To succeed, presidents must not only have a port to seek but they must convince Congress and the electorate that it is a port worth seeking. Politics in a democracy is ultimately an educational process, an adventure in persuasion and consent. Every president stands in Theodore Roosevelt's bully pulpit.

The greatest presidents in the scholars' rankings, Washington, Lincoln, and Franklin Roosevelt, were leaders who confronted and overcame the republic's greatest crises. Crisis widens presidential opportunities for bold and imaginative action. But it does not guarantee presidential greatness. The crisis of secession did not spur Buchanan or the crisis of depression spur Hoover to creative leadership. Their inadequacies in the face of crisis allowed Lincoln and the second Roosevelt to show the difference individuals make to history. Still, even in the absence of first-order crisis, forceful and persuasive presidents—Jefferson, Jackson, Theodore Roosevelt, Ronald Reagan—are able to impose their own priorities on the country.

The diverse drama of the presidency offers a fascinating set of tales. Biographies of American presidents constitute a chronicle of wisdom and folly, nobility and pettiness, courage and cunning, forthrightness and deceit, quarrel and consensus. The turmoil perennially swirling around the White House illuminates the heart of the American democracy.

It is the aim of the American Presidents series to present the grand panorama of our chief executives in volumes compact enough for the busy reader, lucid enough for the student, authoritative enough for the scholar. Each volume offers a distillation of character and career. I hope that these lives will give readers some understanding of the pitfalls and potentialities of the presidency and also of the responsibilities of citizenship. Truman's famous sign—"The buck stops here"—tells only half the story. Citizens cannot escape the ultimate responsibility. It is in the voting booth, not on the presidential desk, that the buck finally stops.

—Arthur M. Schlesinger, Jr.

John Adams

Introduction:
Plato's Wish

In 1813, several years after they had served as presidents of the United States, Thomas Jefferson wrote John Adams expressing hope that the future would bring a "natural aristocracy" arising directly from democracy rather than transmitted by inheritance, an aristocracy based not on birth or wealth but on virtue and talent. Impossible, scoffed Adams. There can be no distinction between a natural and artificial aristocracy when the very category is constructed not by nature but by society's conventions. "Education, Wealth, Strength, Beauty, Stature, Birth, Marriage, graceful Attitudes and Motions, Gait, Complexion, Physiognomy are Talents as well as Genius and Science and learning."

Today such "aristocratic" attributes are enjoyed by athletic heroes, military brave hearts, saintly popes, glitzy billionaires, sashaying fashion models, opera divas, rock stars, and Academy Award winners. Adams warned Jefferson that even a democracy would spawn an aristocratic class capable of commanding attention. Lest we assume that such recognition goes to the young, rich, and beautiful, we should remember what Adams could never forget: The aging, overweight Ben Franklin was lionized in Paris as much for his sexual conquests as his scientific achievements. Madonna would understand. So too some of our contemporary artists, who would settle for celebrity status even if it lasts for only fifteen minutes. But could President Adams, himself driven by "the spur of fame," ever enjoy it?

Some presidents leave the executive office in fame and glory, others in shame and disgrace. Adams left in silence and darkness, at four in the morning, the day his successor was to be sworn in. He left as he entered, perhaps the finest mind ever to be elected to the highest office of the land. A great president?

Bad times make good presidents and worse times great ones. Whatever challenges leaders strengthens them, and a true leader is a born enemy of complacency, one who thrives in a crisis. But normal times without a severe economic depression arouse little concern among the American people. And people are more confused than convinced when they find their country fighting a war militarily while Congress debates declaring it politically (with France, 1798; Mexico, 1848; North Korea, 1950; Vietnam, 1966). Perversely, the best moment redounding to the popularity of a president is when America is attacked (Fort Sumter, 1861; the *Maine*, 1898; the *Lusitania*, 1916; Pearl Harbor, 1941; the World Trade Center, 2001). Short of such historical drama, the presidency is like an act without role or script, and the people an audience viewing a play without plot or purpose, a performance lacking tension, conflict, tragedy, and resolution.

Such was the situation faced by John Adams, the second president of the United States, who served during the formative years of the young republic, 1797 to 1801, long after the Revolution had been gloriously fought and the Constitution wisely established. The late 1790s became a period when leaders were asked to manage government rather than to make history. Thus Adams's brief four years in office seem to stand out as a pathetic parenthesis, a case of character constrained by circumstance. Coming to the presidency after George Washington and followed by Thomas Jefferson, two towering figures who started the "Virginia dynasty" that would be continued by James Madison and James Monroe, Adams was the only one of the first presidents to serve a single term in the executive office. Andrew Jackson, another southerner who identified with Jefferson, also served for a successful two terms (1829–1837), after defeating John Quincy Adams who, like his father, left office after only one term (1825–1829).

In the 1960s, at a dinner in the White House hosting the Nobel

Prize winners in the Western Hemisphere, John F. Kennedy remarked that never before in American history had there been such a gathering of brilliance since Thomas Jefferson dined alone. Would Adams agree?

"I dined a large company once or twice a week; Jefferson dined a dozen every day," Adams growled to Benjamin Rush. "I had levees once a week, that all my time might not be wasted by idle visits. Jefferson's whole eight years was a levee."

American political history begins with the rift between Adams and Jefferson, and it evolved naturally from the psychology of the American founding. The *Federalist* authors, the theoreticians of the Constitution, made not confidence and trust but suspicion and doubt the emotions that would create the possibility of political order, and jealously was seen as the handmaiden of liberty, "a never-sleeping jealously," as Adams put it. Just before they died, Adams and Jefferson embraced each other as "brothers," but in their early political careers the two suspicious minds could only find in each other exactly what they suspected.

Thus Adams distrusted Jefferson as a wasteful aristocrat idling away time on frivolities, and Jefferson suspected Adams himself of scheming to establish the rule of aristocracy in America. Although Jefferson suffered the charge of being a religiously incorrect "non-believer," somehow the Virginian, whose elitist educational ideas would "rake the genius from the rubbish," and whose ideology made the "pursuit of happiness" into a national creed, escaped the charge of aristocracy. Yet historically ease and happiness had been the entitlement of aristocratic society, the leisure class that, as Aristotle put it, could devote itself to civic affairs because it need not bother with the drudgery of labor. "Everything that has been said for heredity," observed Adams's French contemporary Benjamin Constant, "the ancients said for slavery." Jefferson hardly went to work and earned money to purchase slaves; he simply inherited them from his father-in-law, and rather than set them free, as did a few courageous southerners, including Washington, he went along with the rest of the South in turning slaves over to creditors or passing them down through the generations, from family to family. How Jefferson, the heredity-stuck aristocratic slave owner, was able to get away with accusing President Adams of being an "aristo-monocrat" is one of the most notable cases of falsification in American political history.

And what was Adams's terrible offense? It consisted in saying in 1790 what Ralph Waldo Emerson said in 1850 and what today is commonly accepted: Democracy neither can nor should blot out diversity and the distinctions that make a difference—the distinctions of talent, beauty, and strength that the French Revolution set out to obliterate. Curiously Jefferson, who inveighed against the deadening monotony of "uniformity," completely misunderstood what Adams was trying to explain, not the desirability of an inherited aristocracy but the inevitability of a spurious one based on the whims of convention.

Adams's opponents agreed with Tom Paine that society is based on our wants and government on our wickedness. But to Adams, it was the arbitrariness of society that makes the rules of government necessary. Society on its own introduces what today our contemporary postmodernists call the "spectacle of signifiers" and what Adams called "the language of signs," where much of life is ceremony and ritual, simulated rather than real, and what is seen is more important than what can be known and what is written more important than what can be proven. Society is theater, politics performance and spin, and aristocracy is wherever the limelight lands. Society, not government, is the problem, for it is the playground of the passions, of pride and pretense, where the vain demand recognition. Adams wrote about the wanton Romans the way F. Scott Fitzgerald, who had read Petronius, wrote about the wasteful rich and Thorstein Veblen wrote about the leisure class—the idols of useless splendor we shall always have with us. The profoundity of Adams's sensibility lies in his warning that there will be no means of judging society from any religious or transcendental perspective:

A death bed, it is said, shows the emptiness of titles. That may be. But does it not equally show the futility of riches, power, liberty, and all earthly things? "The cloud-capt towers, the gorgeous palaces, the solemn temples, the great globe itself" appear "the baseless fabric of a vision," and "life itself a tale, told by an idiot, full of sound and fury signifying nothing." Shall it be inferred from this, that fame, liberty, property, and life, shall always be despised and neglected? Shall laws and government, which regulate sublunary things, be neglected because they appear baubles at the hour of death?

The prescient Adams saw that in a democratic republic controversies that originate in society move on to the sphere of government and often to the judiciary, the very Constitution that Adams had defended. Society must look beyond itself for judgment, unless it prefers, as Adams and the *Federalist* authors cautioned against, to be a judge in its own cause.

Not only Kennedy but also Presidents Jackson, Lincoln, and Wilson invoked Jefferson's name, as did Franklin D. Roosevelt in the midst of the Great Depression, even when those who opposed his New Deal regarded themselves as staunch Jeffersonians. Public high schools have been named after Jefferson and Washington; except in Massachusetts, few traces of Adams have been left on buildings or monuments, and in history textbooks he is mentioned but rarely treated as a significant figure. In recent years the spectacular popular response to David McCullough's *John Adams*, and an earlier valuable study by Joseph J. Ellis, *Passionate Sage*, has led the U.S. Congress to consider building in the capital a monument to the two Adamses, the second and the sixth presidents. In the 1990s America took to John Adams like a lost soul, the likable curmudgeon who died at ninety-one, on July 4, 1826, gasping in his last breath, seemingly unconcerned with his Maker but instead with his nemesis, "Jefferson still lives!" (Jefferson died on the same day.)

Older than the Constitution's framers, John Adams was involved in every major political crisis from 1765 to 1801. Long before America declared itself independent of England, he provided the reasoning for it. Yet as to President Adams, he is often treated as a brief, passing figure in American political history. In truth, he deserves a far more prominent place in intellectual history and social philosophy. For it is his theory of government that we live with today, although we may be unaware of it. It is also his theory of liberty and rights that survives by virtue of government, even if his own presidency could not survive the conflicting demands made upon it. In Adams, America had the rarest of the species, a president who was not a politician.

The *Federalist* authors, brilliant though they were, and even with their single reference to the need of "energy in the executive," had no idea that the presidency would become America's most important political institution. During Adams's era, European thinkers were enamored of either the "general will" of the people or the sovereignty of Parliament. Adams broke with both traditions to emphasize the importance of the executive. Neither the people nor their representatives have a coherent will nor does sovereignty have a single voice. Only as an idea does "the people" exist, as a representation, not a reality, simply a figure of speech for politicians in search of an audience.

Against both the French Jacobins and the southern Republicans, the opponents of the Federalist Party of Washington and Adams, Adams warned that sovereignty without checks under democracy would be what it had been under monarchy: tyranny, and no less arbitrary than the rule of a king given the vicissitudes of public opinion. The cry "all power to the people" creates the illusion that power will disappear, as though it can be democratized collectively when in reality it expresses itself singularly, not in the deliberation of the many but in the determination of the few. Unless checked, the superior few will try to control, and the democratic many will try to claim. Two conflicting social orders can be balanced only by the presence of a third institution, the executive. Treasury secretary Alexander Hamilton also believed in a strong executive, but he looked upon the "rich, well-born, and able" with trust; Adams looked upon elites with suspicion.

When Adams's critics told him that people can be counted upon to be on their own because their love for freedom is so great, Adams replied that lions also love their freedom and feel no need to be governed. He was fond of quoting Shakespeare: "Power into will, will into appetite / And appetite an universal wolf." Only government can control "the fever whereof all power is sick."

But what Adams believed Jefferson disdained. "That government is best which governs least," declared Jefferson, who trusted popular sovereignty to leave people alone and free to run their own lives. Such a formulation may have left Americans alone all right, but it also left them with a legacy that was as much a curse as a blessing: America was left facing the incompatibility of popular sovereignty with natural right, the will of the majority with the ability of minorities or individuals to enjoy freedom and self-determination. The Founders held that people do not have a right to do wrong, and Jefferson hoped that what was "rightful" would be "reasonable." But democracy's cult of a free people's infallible will became the rationale used to justify expanding slavery into the western territories as well as excluding immigrants from participating in the democratic dream. Adams discerned the contradiction that resides within liberty and democracy, the tension between unalienable rights and their threat by the rule of popular opinion. But America voted Adams out of office and went on to live with a theoretical time bomb that exploded on the battlefield of the Civil War.

Historians are reluctant to give Adams a higher rating than Jefferson in evaluating their respective presidencies. But when one studies their attitudes toward the meaning and fate of liberty, both in America and during the French Revolution and the slave uprising in Haiti, there can be no doubt that Adams is the better educator. Revolutionary France saw itself as radically innovative in all things, including the invention of the guillotine. The revolution was made in the name of "Reason," "Virtue," and "The People," and Jefferson cheered it on, the execution of the king and queen and the bloody Terror itself. Death by guillotine, observed the philosopher G. W. F. Hegel, was "the coldest and meanest of all deaths, with no more significance than cleaving off a head of cabbage or swallowing a draught of water." The deaths troubled Jefferson a little but not much. "The liberty of the whole earth was depending on the issue of the contest," he wrote in 1793, "and was ever such a prize won with so little innocent blood?" Against the crusading revolutionary exuberance of Jefferson and Tom Paine, who also believed that heads must fall so that freedom may rise, Adams sought to keep things in perspective. "Ours was a revolution against innovation," he emphasized, reminding Americans that the "spirit of '76" was meant to preserve old freedoms, not to propagate new fictions.

Adams discerned what his opponents denied and Lincoln had to face: A republican form of government is no guarantee that people will respect the rights of others. Jefferson and Paine saw themselves as revolutionists and insisted that people have a right to do what they will do; Adams saw himself as a constitutionalist and insisted that "laws are intended not to trust to what men will do, but to guard against what they might do."

The Jefferson-Adams dualism culminated in the Lincoln-Douglas debates of 1858. Senator Stephen Douglas invoked the doctrine of popular sovereignty to claim that the people of Kansas and Nebraska had a right to vote for or against slavery as they saw fit. Lincoln replied that popular sovereignty undermined the Declaration of Independence and left it "without the *germ* or even *suggestion* of the individual rights of man," thereby rendering it "mere rubbish" and "old wadding." Although Lincoln reasoned with Adams to get us out of a contradiction, when it came to speeches on the Fourth of July, he hailed Jefferson, the president who left us with the contradiction!

Adams saw politics as the dramatization of two drives: the desire to dominate and the desire to be free of domination. As Adams warned, America's aversion to government would render political authority so weak it could do little to interfere with the predatory drives of America's "artificial aristocracy," and hence democracy's cherished masses are at the mercy of elites and their will to power.

While Adams perceived government as a reflection of human nature and its conflicting drives, his antagonists assumed that as government grows democracy withers. In the course of American history, that assumption turned out to be just the opposite, with democratic participation giving rise to the state as people look to it to do for them what they cannot do for themselves (to use Lincoln's formulation). Adams's prescient modernism lies in his insight that the existence of freedom itself by no means rids the world of the possibility of domination. Even before the French Revolution broke out, Adams predicted that a democratic assembly without countervailing chambers could be a prescription for domination. "Mixed together, in equal halves, the nobles will forever tyrannize."

Looking to the structure of government to control class domination, President Adams viewed the state as an instrument of justice. There is, it should be remembered, no role for the state in Jefferson's heralded Declaration of Independence. A document of dissolution that announced the colonies' bold separation from the mother country, the Declaration left America sovereign but stranded. For without the political institutions that Adams had championed, a strong executive, a national judiciary, and a military, the Declaration would have remained little more than a scrap of paper. All the progressive causes in American history—from the rights of labor to the struggles of women and ethnic minorities— required the authority of the state for their realization. Ironically, the egalitarian ideals Jefferson espoused would be realized in the very institutions he opposed.

Adams saw government functioning as means not only of preserving liberty but also of exercising authority without which human rights cannot be realized, protected, and perpetuated. His antigovernment opponents rejected the authority of the past as well as that of the state, agreeing with Paine that government is founded on the false shame of sin, "the badge of lost innocence," whereas society is the arena of harmony and hope. For Adams, a distinction between state and society cannot so easily be made since the institutions of the former are designed to deal with the impulses of the latter. Adams was almost obsessed not only with government but with its precise forms and functions since history stood as a taunt to America's aspirations. The story of republicanism, of those political regimes that tried to exist without a monarchy, is the story of systematic failure, the record not of survival and success but of decline and fall. Older republics rose proudly, only to disappear from history, sinking with the trace of tears, full of splash and fury signifying nothing. All the republics of the ancient world and those of the Middle Ages and the Renaissance city-states, Adams took pains to remind America, had "foamed, raged, and burst, like so many water spouts upon the ocean."

John Adams remains an enigma entangled in ironies. Consider

the portraits: Adams the last voice of classical republicanism holding forth as though wearing a Roman toga; the first modernist who
presages with "anthropological realism" that behavior is characterized more by primitive rivalry than by classical harmony; the political scientist impatient with politics and disdainful of political
parties; the intrepid unifier determined to put nation ahead of sec-
tion; the patient diplomat of neutrality in a world of bipolarity when
America had to choose between France and England in a time of war
hysteria; the cold cynic calmly allowing the Alien and Sedition Acts
to portend a "reign of terror"; the paragon of probity as faithful to
the Bible as he was to his wife, Abigail; the erratic executive, at once
touchy, impulsive, impassioned; the president who left town to go
home to Quincy, leaving cabinet members wondering if he was ever
coming back. Perhaps the only sure generalization that can be made
about John Adams is that we shall never see his likes again.

A study of President John Adams raises the question of leadership
and citizenship in a democracy. In his few years in office Adams
would gladly have led America, if only the American people had
known where they wanted to go with their new experiment in self-
government. Would the young country follow the more demanding
ideals of New England and rise to civic responsibility, or would it
settle for the easy life of the South and the quest for comfort and
pleasure? The New England–born Adams could be wickedly witty
and often enjoyed a quaff of Madeira, but he was not one to be
seduced by ease. Throughout his life he was insecure about his reputation and he hungered after recognition and distinction. To be
noticed, admired, and esteemed, Adams felt, was the ruling passion
not just of himself but of human nature in general. America, alas,
scarcely noticed the one president who came closest to fulfilling
Plato's wish to see a philosopher in power.

   The ancient Greek thinker insisted that a republic must be governed by the wisdom of philosophy or it may very well not be governed at all. His successor Aristotle agreed, convinced that reason
could tame the passions so that citizens would know the good and
leaders would do it. Adams, however, rejected the elitist "dogma of
Aristotle," which privileged the chattering leisure class that gathered

around the *polis* to the "tyrannical exclusion" of all others in enjoying the ranks and rights of citizenship. Adams took upon himself
"the severe task of going through all" of Plato's works, "with the
help of two Latin translations," and "comparing some of the
remarkable passages with the Greek." He appreciated Plato's discussions of the forms of government and the passions of the people.
But he remarked that the history of Greece could function as a
"boudoir," an octagonal room with high mirrors on every wall and
everywhere a person turns he will see his misshapened body, a sight
that may help him recover his temper. Later he jested to Jefferson
that the only really important thing he learned from the Greek
thinker was the profound truth that "sneezing was a cure for hick-
ups." After reading Plato, Adams would carry in his pocket a pinch
of snuff for his cabinet meetings.

Although Adams wrote a massive treatise defending the U.S.
Constitution against its European critics, there was no place for him
within it as an intellectual. "In a nation of philosophers," the *Federalist* authors wrote, one could count upon the people to abide by
the Constitution and the precepts of legality, for in that case "a rev-
erence for the law would be sufficiently inculcated by the voice of
enlightened reason. But a nation of philosophers is as little to be
expected as the philosophical race of kings wished for by Plato."
Nor can America rely upon the worthiest and wisest to turn up
later to lead the country and render the clash of interests sub-
servient to the public good. Why not? "Enlightened statesmen will
not always be at the helm." Adams himself concurred. "I have long
been settled in my opinion," he wrote to Jefferson in 1787, "that
neither Philosophy, nor Religion, nor Morality, nor Wisdom, nor
Interest, will ever govern nations or Parties, against their Vanity,
their Pride, their Resentment or Revenge, or their Avarice or Ambition. Nothing but Force and Power and Strength can restrain them."

Combine Adams's philosophical reflections with his political
aspirations, and what do we get? A formula for frustration. While
he doubted that the people had a capacity to think rationally and to
act virtuously, he would see himself as doing so, only to wonder
why he went unappreciated in a democracy of the unenlightened.
Jefferson, in contrast, simply told the people what they wanted to

hear and not necessarily what they needed to know. Adams agreed with the *Federalist* authors that Plato's wish would be unfulfilled and America would not be "a nation of philosophers." Jefferson told his followers that the "ploughman" was wiser than philosophers and professors combined, convinced that the masters of the physical environment would guide the young republic and that Americans were the salt of the earth, "the chosen people of God." As president, Adams had to ask the "chosen people" if they would please pay taxes so America might defend itself in the event of war. He would not be reelected.

The historian Henry Adams, the great-grandson of John Adams, once quipped that the evolution of the presidency from George Washington to Ulysses Grant disproves Darwin's theory of the progress of the human species. On March 3, 1901, the date of the centennial of John Adams's last day as president of the United States, Henry Adams wrote to Elizabeth Cameron from his residence in Washington, D.C. "I look over to the White House wondering what my old friend Thomas Jefferson would say. It is just a hundred years since he turned my harmless ancestor into the street at midnight."

The Adams legacy is one of the greatest gifts a family ever made to American history. But America rebuked John Adams. A dozen years after Adams had left the presidency, his friend Benjamin Rush assured him that even his opponents never questioned his "integrity" and believed him to be an "honest man." Adams remained unassuaged, reminding Rush that he had been charged with attempting to make his son his successor and hence saddling America with hereditary monarchy. "Washington and Franklin could never do anything but what was imputed to pure, disinterested patriotism; I could never do anything but what was ascribed to sinister motives." Typically, Adams was hard on himself. Even though he can scarcely be called an event-making president or one who changed the course of history, those who knew Adams, including some of his enemies, felt themselves in the presence of a rare and virtuous character.

Rather small, barely five foot seven, portly and thick shouldered, sporting a bag wig that curled over the ears, a large round head from which peered eyes that changed with his emotions, from a vehement stare to a joyous twinkle, John Adams carried the promises and paradoxes of America's political culture within himself. He could explode with masculine pugnacity and emote with feminine sensitivity. Regarding political behavior as collective in nature, he chose to stand alone as an individual. He desired to be well liked, but he refused to suffer fools gladly. He sought to impress the public but had distinctly unimpressive physical features, with stubby legs that seemed barely able to support a stout carriage; he was so short that when he wore a sword, as he did on ceremonial occasions, it sometimes scratched the steps when he went up stairs. In later life without a wig, Adams had a bald dome rounded with a thick gob of hair, a worn face with jowls resting on a small, prim mouth, and a body inclining to corpulence. So endowed, Adams craved fame yet despised public opinion, perplexed that his robust honesty won him respect but not popularity. He delighted in social conversation and hated politics, and he believed in the efficacy of political institutions but not in the necessity of political parties. He articulated a political philosophy based on doubt, suspicion, and distrust, only to emerge as one of the most trusting presidents ever to sit in the executive office, so trusting he was unaware his cabinet was working against him.

Early American political culture involved a struggle among three competing visions. Jefferson looked to the many, Hamilton to the few, and Adams the one, that is, a strong executive who would mediate between the democratic masses and a wealthy aristocracy. Although Adams worried about the turbulence of democracy as much as the arrogance of aristocracy, it was the pretensions of the latter that occupied his political philosophy, for Adams believed then what social theorists know only now: that the masses endow wealth with authority and seek to emulate its every gesture and fashion. Equally skeptical of Jefferson's democracy as well as Hamilton's plutocracy, Adams looked to the executive to assure that government serves neither the many nor the few but the public good at large. Thus he entered the presidency assuming that if he conducted himself fairly, justly, and independently, he would enjoy the respect and trust he deserved.

Ben Franklin described Adams as "always an honest Man, often a Wise One, but sometimes and in somethings, absolutely out of his Senses." Adams joined the ranks of other moralists also regarded as lacking common sense for believing that ideals, however unrealizable, are not to be violated and principles, however difficult to sustain, are not to be compromised. It was Franklin, after all, who sought compromise with England in order to reconcile the colonies with the monarchy. As the Revolution approached, Adams stood adamant by independence, a stubborn, indomitable spirit that gave courage to the colonists to aspire to the impossible and not to submit and yield during a trying time as a fresh new republic was struggling to be born.

The presidency of John Adams dramatized, perhaps more than any other in American history, the tension between ethics and power, integrity and success, conviction and compromise. After Adams the American presidency would find it difficult to adhere to unswerving principles as each political party adopted whatever program promised to bring electoral victory. Adams had hoped to make the presidency "independent," but government itself would become interdependent on voters and money, and the American people would adhere to no theory of government other than to have it respond to what they wanted it to do or not to do.

No less than Adams did Jefferson value "independence" and self-reliant individualism. "Dependence begets subservience and venality," Jefferson warned, "suffocates the germ of virtue, and prepares fit tools for the designs of ambition." Jefferson claimed that when he defeated Adams in the election of 1800, he saved America from aristocracy and monarchy, little realizing that his utter reliance on party politics represented a defeat of his own ideals. An indulgent consumer who came to be dependent upon his creditors, a plantation owner who depended on the labor of his slaves, Jefferson also became a politician dependent on a political party to serve his political purposes. Politics would now dominate a government less concerned with civic virtue and the public good than with the next election. American history would discover what Adams had learned and the historian Henry Adams would have us remember: Not the president's idea of virtue but people's idea of interests decides whether Americans wish to live for government, against government, or off government. Politics begets dependency, smothers the spark of virtue, and prepares America to ask little of itself and less of its leaders. The relationship of democracy to the people, John Adams observed, with the famous novel of Samuel Richardson in mind, is that of the cruel passions of a rake who drives his fiancée to suicide. "Democracy is Lovelace, and the people are Clarissa. The artful villain will pursue the innocent young girl to her ruin and death." Seduced only to be betrayed, the people need to be protected, even from democracy itself.

Adams lived long enough to understand that Jefferson's hedonistic settling for happiness and its desires would take the place of his own heroic appeals to government and its duties. "The first want of man is his dinner, and the second his girl," observed Adams, who also recognized that "no appetite in human nature is more universal than that for honor," only to realize that in democratic politics honor goes to the victorious and not to the virtuous. With success the single standard of judgment in America's culture—"the bitch-goddess of success," as the philosopher William James put it—professional politics took on the motto of professional football: winning isn't everything; it's the only thing. Adams was far from a winner, but what America lost in his losing can only be regretted until it is regained: a politics of conscience hounded by a fear of guilt and hallowed by a love of truth.

1

From "Senseless Turpitude"
to Stately Duty

FATHER AND SON

John Adams was born in Braintree, Massachusetts, on October 19, 1735, the fourth-generation descendant of Henry Adams, who arrived in America with his wife, Edith, about 1636. Of yeoman stock, pious, frugal, and hardworking, Henry died a decade after settling in Braintree, leaving eight sons and a daughter, a house with two rooms, a farm of forty acres on which ranged a cow, heffer, and swine, and a modest library of treasured books. One son, Joseph, followed in his father's footsteps and, married to Abigail Baxter, had no less than twelve children. Their son Joseph Adams Jr. married Hannah Bass, great-granddaughter of John and Priscilla Alden of the Plymouth landing and *Mayflower* epic. Their son, the first John Adams, married Susanna Boylston, the daughter of a family in Massachusetts medical history. Into the Adams-Boylston marriage was born John Adams, the eldest of the three sons.

The dwelling in which young Adams grew up was plain, simple, severe. On the farm of hay fields sat a two-story clapboard house with a single chimney that served to heat four dimly lit rooms. The sloping roof made the two upstairs bedrooms into a low cubbyhole under which the boys had to stoop to turn in to bed. As with much of the rest of Puritan New England, the Adams family experienced life as a challenge to moral character, an austere, demanding existence without the luxury of servants or slaves.

Although lacking material comfort and often enduring dreary

weather, the Adams household enjoyed a wealth of books, ideas, and stimulating conversation. A theological atmosphere weighed down upon New England, with citizens worrying about the fate of their souls while debating the inscrutability of God's purposes and the meaning of evil. Adams senior took his son to a barnlike meetinghouse to hear sermons asking the congregation to turn to faith, and then to the town meeting to hear public issues discussed that asked citizens to rely upon reason. The father hoped his eldest son would enter college and study for the ministry. But young Adams was not the bookworm that one might assume in view of his later life as a learned intellectual. He relished the outdoors; knew every trail, pond, and woods in the neighborhood; and took pride in his physical prowess despite his small size. Well into adulthood he would retain a passion for tracking and hunting. His father, however, a farmer and outdoorsman himself, wanted his son to study Latin to prepare for Harvard College. When he protested that he hated the subject, his father replied: "Well, John, if Latin-grammar does not suit you, you may try ditching, perhaps that will; my meadow yonder needs a ditch, and you may put by Latin and try that." Young John looked forward to the "delightful change," only to discover after a day and a half of hard, backbreaking work that he preferred Latin to labor. But he felt too humiliated to admit it to his father. Finally at nightfall "toil conquered pride, and I told my father, one of the severest trials of my life, that, if he chose, I would go back to Latin-grammar. He was glad of it; and if I have since gained any distinction, it has been owing to the two days' labor in that abominable ditch."

Adams entered Harvard at fifteen. To the Puritan founders of New England, the life of the mind was everything; few could forget that the doctrines of the Protestant Reformation were first promulgated in the universities of Europe. Under Harvard's tutorial system, Adams studied Greek and Latin, logic, rhetoric, physics, and, in his senior year, moral philosophy and metaphysics. Not all his classmates buckled down. Some of Harvard's brightest students would be reprimanded for drinking, gambling, rioting, whoring, and, even worse, lapses into infidelity and blasphemy. Adams was reticent about his college experience. Perhaps his lack of enthusiasm reflected the rote nature of the learning that had students simply copying the contents of books rather than critically analyzing them. In his later years, Adams would do both when subjecting Western political philosophy to his penetrating analysis, quoting long passages from Machiavelli to show where the Florentine political philosopher contradicts himself.

Adams was graduated from Harvard in 1755, and returned to Braintree uncertain of a vocation. The ministry that his father favored Adams found stifling. He had his fill of the doctrinal disputes surrounding "frigid John Calvin," and he could not help remembering the attacks on the liberal theologian Jonathan Mayhew and others who deviated from orthodoxy. He decided to accept an earlier offer of a teaching position at a grammar school in Worcester, and with a horse sent by the town for him to ride, he made the sixty-mile trip from Braintree (later called Quincy) in a single day.

The opportunity to teach young people led Adams to reflect upon what it is that motivates the mind. Who in the class will turn out to be a "hero" or a "rake" or a "philosopher" or a "parasite"? The boredom and daydreaming of the students rubbed off on the schoolmaster, who found his own mind wandering out the window. Schoolteachers were poorly paid, and Adams could only afford to board with families. It was in his first few years as a Worcester instructor that Adams started to keep a diary. The opening pages are full of doubt, self-scrutiny, and intellectual curiosity about God and the nature of the universe and the adequacy of his own character. "Constantly forming but never executing good resolutions," he lamented. "Oh! That I could wear out my mind any mean and base affectation; conquer my natural pride and self-conceit; expect no more deference from my fellows than I deserve; . . . subdue every unworthy passion, and treat all men as I wish to be treated by all." What troubled Adams was that his mind flitted with thoughts that seemed to have no object, leaving his mental life all motion and no direction. And his inability to concentrate resulted in many students' dilemma:

What is the Cause of Procrastination? To day my Stomack is Disordered, and my Thoughts of Consequences, unsteady and Confused. I cant study to day but will begin tomorrow. Tomorrow comes. Well, I feel pretty well, my head is pretty clear, but Company comes in. I cant yet study tomorrow, but will begin in Earnest next day. Next day comes. We are out of Wood, I cant study: because I cant keep a fire. Thus, something is always wanting that is necessary.

Adams's experience in the classroom led him to believe that young minds are more likely to be motivated positively than negatively, by expectations of praise instead of fear of punishment. At this point in his life, having turned twenty-one and finding himself still uncertain of his chosen vocation, Adams became preoccupied with motivation. In view of his later social philosophy, which would emphasize the human need for external recognition, his earlier thoughts valued even more the force of inner conviction. In 1756, he wrote to a friend, "Upon common theatres, indeed, the applause of the audience is of more importance to the actor than their own approbation. But upon the stage of life, while conscience claps, let the world hiss." But Adams's conscience was hardly clapping as he sank into idleness, the worst sin for a Puritan. "I am dull and inactive, and all my resolutions, all the spirits I can muster are insufficient to rouse me from this senseless turpitude." He knew he had to leave behind grammar-school teaching, and he thought about the three options available to college graduates: divinity, medicine, or law. Against the advice of family and friends, he chose to study law, then a profession of mixed repute.

The original settlers of New England had no lawyers. But when the visions of commonwealth and love quickly receded, and conflict and distrust took hold, the profession of law emerged to handle suits and litigations. Public as well as personal disputations shaped the life of law, and indeed the controversies between the colonies and mother country that led to the Revolution were legal in nature. Adams would argue the American cause as a lawyer, defending a country whose rights had been violated. Adams carried into his new chosen calling the religious idealism that sprang from his Puritan environment. A century later Adams's great-grandson Henry Adams would look upon the legal profession as the hireling of big business. But "honest John Adams" saw law as an instrument of morality, and he dedicated himself to the profession as a cause that fulfilled his need to do right by his conscience.

Adams was cut out perfectly for the profession. He delighted in courtroom drama; enjoyed riding the circuit; had a clear, sonorous manner of speaking, a mind that could cut quickly to the heart of an issue and present effective summations, and a character so open in its convictions that few could suspect him of concealing evidence or manipulating opinion. He valued law as rooted in history, in experience, and in precedent. Admitted to the bar by the Massachusetts Superior Court in 1761, Adams returned to Braintree and out of a small office handled matters dealing with property, taxes, deeds, and wills; while on the circuit he took cases involving theft, libel, rape, and bastardy. In his hometown he also led a crusade against taverns, whose customers took to drinking and brawling. Adams succeeded in getting an ordinance to limit the licensing of these dens of iniquity, appearing in court in his distinguished black robe and white wig.

Adams was particularly impressed by the stirring role of another lawyer. James Otis took to court the case of Boston merchants protesting the breaking into of their ships and warehouses by British customs officials whose actions had been authorized by writs of assistance issued by the English Crown. Otis's speech against the writs deeply moved Adams. The trial itself involved only a petty matter of protecting smugglers, but it would have, Adams reflected, implications for the limitations of British authority in America. From the courtroom resonated the theory of the social compact stipulating the natural rights of citizens and the right of revolution itself.

ABIGAIL AND THE "WILD AND GIDDY DAYS"

Long before he was a practicing attorney, Adams felt himself drawn to the female sex. His wit and charm appealed to village belles, and while he himself remained chaste, Braintree and other towns had their share of unwed mothers and bastard children. Male friends warned him against the tender trap of matrimony, and few rushed into it at an early age. Even so, Adams spent hours "gallanting the girls" and reading Ovid to the wife of the town doctor. He found himself captivated by the enticing Hannah Quincy, who had other young men swarming around her like moths to a flame. On one occasion he almost proposed to her, but friends burst into the room and the embarrassed couple drew apart. When Hannah soon after married another suitor, Adams suddenly knew what it meant to be lovesick, unable to sleep without thinking of her beautiful smiling face, a scene that aroused desires that could not be fulfilled and lingered only to "be grappled to my soul. Wherever I go, whatever I do, asleep or awake, This dear bewitching scene attends me, and takes up all my Thoughts."

One of Adams's best friends married in 1761, two years after he first met Abigail Smith. But Adams put off becoming engaged to Abigail until early 1764. Unlike the flirtatious Hannah, Abigail, then only fifteen and ten years younger than Adams, was too coy to show her feelings to the man who moved her heart, and it took him some time to sense her rare qualities of mind and spirit. He also felt inadequate financially, having no prospects of becoming rich. But with the death of his father he inherited a saltbox cottage on the farm, and after three years he grew confident and pursued her ardently. His instincts proved correct. The forty-five-year marriage between John and Abigail Adams constitutes one of the great romances in the history of the American presidency. The relationship was a rapture of fused souls. They came together, John said, "like magnet and steel." But political duty took John away for long stays in Europe, and during the twelve years when he was vice president and president, Abigail frequently remained in Quincy. Until Adams left office in 1801, he and Abigail had lived apart more often than together. But correspondence between the two sustained an intimacy that age could not wither. Earlier, when Adams was serving as a diplomat in Europe, Abigail expressed her feelings before leaving to join him: "My thoughts are fixed, my latest wish depend / on thee guide, guardian, Husband, lover, Friend." It was the rarest of relationships, one in which husband and wife were exceptionally well mated, and love conquered space and time.

Abigail came from the town of Weymouth, born into a well-off ministerial family whose members thought her marriage to a small-town lawyer was beneath her. As a youth, Abigail had suffered from frequent illnesses, although she thought back fondly on a pleasant childhood of "wild and giddy days." Together with her two sisters, she received her education at home with her mother serving as instructor and her father's library as a valuable resource. Well-read, perceptive, witty, Abigail carried on with John Adams as an equal, bringing stability to his dark moods and self-doubts. A painting, rendered around the time of the marriage, shows her with a serenely attractive face from which stare dark, intense eyes; hair pulled back; and lips about to smile but holding the serious look customary in eighteenth-century portraits. Later drawings show her aging gracefully. In some of her letters she took the pen name "Portia," reference to the long-suffering wife of the Roman leader Brutus. But Abigail was whimsical rather than whining. She never complained of marriage and motherhood but instead accepted the conventional code of female behavior while valuing her own privacy and autonomy. With her husband occupied with public life, Abigail took on the responsibility of managing the farm and handling financial matters. She also became a gifted letter writer, carrying on a rich correspondence not only with her husband but with the author Mercy Otis Warren, one of the first historians of the American Revolution.

After the Revolution broke out there were moments when Abigail did become political. In the spring of 1776, she wrote to John: "I long to hear that you have declared an independency," and she then offered the advice, "and by the way in the new Code of Laws which I suppose it will be necessary for you to make I desire you would Remember the Ladies, and be more generous and favorable to them than your ancestors." She concluded her counsel with sentiments common to colonial women. "Do not put such unlimited power in the hands of the Husbands. Remember all men would be tyrants if they could."

"THE MOST MAGNIFICENT MOVEMENT OF ALL":
THE REVOLUTION

In 1763, a seven-year war between England and France for the control of North America came to an end, the so-called French and Indian War that saw native Americans fighting alongside France in the Northeast, where "New France" went down to defeat with the fall of Quebec. "This," said the English statesman Lord Granville, "has been the most glorious war and the most triumphant peace that England ever knew." Granville uttered that thought on his deathbed; fortunately, he would not live to see how wrong he was. In less than two decades, England would be driven out of America, and not by France or Spain but by her own children.

England's victory created two ironic circumstances. While the American colonists no longer felt they needed England for protection against the French and native Indians, England just as strongly believed it needed America to pay for the war and the upkeep of the colonial system as well as the security afforded by the British army and navy. The century-old relationship of America to the mother country had been characterized by charters, laws, and regulations, many of which were so ill defined and ignored that an English historian remarked that his country's relations with the world and the settlement of America took place in a "fit of absence of mind." To rectify the situation, the British Parliament passed the Stamp Act of 1765. The legislation, requiring all kinds of printed material, from newspapers to diplomas to legal documents, to carry revenue seals, meant that for the first time in history colonists had been taxed directly. When news of the law reached America in May, Boston exploded in anger. Tax collectors were tarred and feathered, stamp seals seized and burned, effigies hung and bonfires lit, and the house of Peter Oliver, Lieutenant Governor Thomas Hutchinson's brother-in-law, was stormed and smashed into shambles; soon after, Hutchinson's own luxurious house full of paintings, silver, china, and rare books was gutted.

The behavior of the once law-abiding Boston people troubled Adams. Those who led the assaults called themselves the "Sons of

Liberty," but Adams wondered whether liberty could survive the passions of a mob riot. Adams and a dozen leading citizens organized an evening club to discuss the meaning of law and order in a political culture based on rights and freedoms. Out of these discussions came Adams's first contribution to political philosophy, *A Dissertation on the Canon and Feudal Law*. The essays were published anonymously and without title in the Boston *Gazette* and later appeared in London. The document, much discussed at the time, has since fallen into neglect. A pity, for Adams, like Abraham Lincoln later in American history, was attempting to explain the meaning of America to America and to the world.

When English men, women, and children departed from the Old World to come to the New, they brought with them the best single idea and left behind the two worst. They arrived with the germ of the idea of the natural rights of humankind and left back in the Old World the ideas of absolutism and dogmatism based on the institutions of feudalism and Catholicism, the reign of "kings and cruel priests." Both feudal and canon law kept their subjects in a state of "sordid ignorance and staring timidity," and it was only with the Protestant Reformation, whose rebellious spirit the Puritans brought to America, that there took place a world-shaking revolt against the tyranny of church and state. The *Dissertation* signaled Adams's most radical moment when he seemed to be questioning authority in the name of liberty and obedience in the name of resistance. He was trying to make America aware of that which Edmund Burke would later try to make the British Parliament aware: the colonists as Protestants are by nature implacable protesters who will not be subdued, but instead will suspect the worst if anyone tries to infringe upon their sovereignty. King George III may call the colonists "rebels," but they are rebels with a cause and a conscience. The great sin, announced Adams the Puritan, is passivity and complacency. "Let us dare to read, think, speak, and write."

Due to the protests of Adams and others, England repealed the Stamp Act, and the colonists rejoiced. But in 1767, Parliament proposed new legislation imposing duties on goods imported to the colonies, insisting that the tax was external rather than internal in that it involved foreign trade. Once again, Adams argued against any form of taxation without consent and representation. While Parliament debated the new duties law, England increased the number of troops in America. Colonists taunted British soldiers, "Bloody Lobsterbacks," and a youth was killed by a musket shot. Shortly after the boy's funeral, a gang of youths flung rocks at soldiers and dared them to use their guns. When the mob shouted "Kill them!," shots rang out, leaving three men dead and eight wounded. One of the dead was a brave, brawny mulatto, Crispus Attucks, who had joined the whites in baiting the troops, the first African American to die in the cause of American freedom.

The officer who allegedly gave the order to fire, Captain Thomas Preston, was arrested and turned over to the city's Superior Court to be tried for the "Boston Massacre." British officers prevailed upon Adams to defend Preston, and when he accepted the case, the people of Boston could only wonder whether he was truly committed to the patriots' cause. Adams and another attorney, Josiah Quincy, produced witnesses who testified that the captain and his terrified soldiers had been provoked into firing. But to dramatize the fear, Adams resorted to an early form of racial profiling, reminding the jury that the mob was "a motley rabble of saucy boys, Negroes and mullatoes, Irish teagues [pigs] and outlandish jack tars," and that the troops faced the African Attucks, whose "very looks" would "terrify any person." He also made a powerful case for self-defense. The British were acquitted.

The American Revolution began in mischief. What has come to be called the Boston Tea Party of December 16, 1773, started when patriots dressed as Indians boarded British ships and quietly dropped overboard 365 chests of tea. Adams, hearing the dramatic story from Abigail, wrote exultantly in his diary of "the most magnificent movement of all," so courageous that there is "a dignity, a majesty, a sublimity" on the part of the patriots who stole aboard British ships in the Boston Harbor and, under cover of darkness, staged the party that made history. "This destruction of the tea is so bold, so daring, so firm, intrepid and inflexible, and it must have so important consequences, and so lasting, that I can't but consider it as an epoch in history!" More than an act of vandalism, the destruction of property symbolized the point of no return. "The die is cast," Adams wrote to a friend.

England felt the same way and ordered the port of Boston closed. Then rumors began arriving from England that Redcoats were coming, that patriot leaders had been indicted for treason, or, better news, that the tea duty had been revoked. Some leaders, including Ben Franklin, urged caution and tried to explore the possibility of compromise. The leader of the faction that would come to be known as the "Loyalists," Daniel Leonard, went so far as to insist that the colonists had no right to oppose taxes and to defy the authority of the mother country. Leonard also charged inconsistency. At the time of the Stamp Act the colonists had acknowledged that England could levy taxes to regulate trade for the purpose of promoting commercial advantages but could not do so solely to raise revenue. When that law was repealed and new legislation was proposed on tea and other commodities, the colonists denied all forms of taxation, whether internal or external. Leonard also charged that a small clique of agitators was misleading the colonists and inflaming them with the suspicion that England intended not only to regulate the colonies but to subvert the people's rights and liberties. Adams replied to Leonard and other Tory voices in a series of papers that appeared in the Boston *Gazette* with the title "Novanglus," Latin for New England. The rebels could read Adams's writings as a powerful justification of their cause; they can also be read in hindsight as a rationalization.

Adams displayed considerable erudition in drawing upon the teachings of "Aristotle and Plato, Livy and Cicero, and Sidney, Harrington and Locke," whose thoughts were grounded in the "principles of nature and eternal reason." But "Novanglus" is more polemical than profound. Of the authors cited, only John Locke regarded people as endowed with the right of revolution; the others could be cited, as indeed they were, to uphold England's position that reason and virtue commanded the colonists to subordinate their interests to the greater good of the commonwealth. Adams's essays anticipated the Declaration of Independence in rejecting any right whatsover of Parliament to rule in the colonies. Both documents were declarations of freedom that sprang from the deeper emotion of denial, rejecting the authority to which colonists once swore allegiance. The American Revolution, it turned out, would be less a war of ideas than a power struggle between a mother country determined to prevail and her colonies determined to be free. Adams may have invoked the "principles of nature and eternal reason," but he well knew that the dispute would be settled by brute force. If Great Britain dared to subordinate the colonies to Parliament, she must do so by "the law of brickbats and balls, which can be answered only by brickbats and balls."

Before the last of the "Novanglus" papers were published, gunfire was indeed answered by gunfire. On the fields of Concord and Lexington, on April 19, 1775, power replaced philosophy, and the issue of sovereignty would be determined not by reason but by strength. Taking positions behind trees, colonial minutemen exchanged volleys with British Redcoats and harassed their retreat to Boston. War, at last, had broken out, but it would take more than a year for America to declare its independence from England. In that period an epidemic of smallpox swept through the northern colonies, taking its toll on thousands of British and American soldiers and leaving Abigail Adams to care for a household of sick children. Boston became a hospital.

The Revolution saw the colonies deeply divided. In Adams's estimate, one-third of the people supported the Revolution, one-third opposed it, and one-third were neutral or indifferent. Pennsylvania Quakers had no stomach for war, and some Virginians thought England could be persuaded to change its policies. Many delegates to the Continental Congress were instructed by their states not to vote for independence. Rumors speculated about sending a peace commission to England. Adams knew that ties with England had been forever broken. He also knew that it would be a long war and that other countries would be reluctant to recognize America until it became sovereign and independent. But America hesitated to take that bold step. Then in January 1776, a small pamphlet came forth from a side-street printer in Philadelphia, and Americans suddenly knew what had to be done.

Thomas Paine's *Common Sense* swept the colonies with its powerfully simple message. It is absurd, Paine insisted, for an island to presume to govern a continent. Indeed, government itself, "the badge of lost innocence," is an artificial inconvenience based on our vices when in the New World all that is needed is a society of liberty and open opportunity. America offered the world a fresh start if it would only seize the moment and come to a "final separation." The sun shines on our cause. "The birthday of a new world is at hand."

As did much of America, Adams welcomed Paine's propitious pamphlet. Yet while its spectacular popularity helped the cause of independence, Adams worried that Paine's pamphleteering approach to political thought would ill prepare America for a true understanding of what would be needed in the postrevolutionary era. Thus again he reached for his pen and wrote *Thoughts on Government*. Paine, Adams observed to Abigail, displays more talent in tearing down government than in having any thought on how it should be set up. Drawing upon classical sources, Adams insisted that happiness is founded only in virtue, and the people's capacity for virtue depends on the deliberate structure and administration of government, a government of institutions and laws and not simply of people acting on their own with neither rules nor restraints. Adams's thoughts circulated throughout the thirteen colonies at a time when each was deciding on establishing its own state government.

On July 2, 1776, Adams was appointed to a five-man committee to frame resolutions that would announce: "That these United Colonies are, and of Right ought to be, Free and Independent States." How the actual draft of the Declaration of Independence came to be written by Jefferson remains unclear. Adams claimed he chose Jefferson as the better writer. Although Jefferson cannot remember Adams's claim, the author did indeed compose a forceful and felicitous manifesto. And while Jefferson supplied the language that made the case for independence, Adams supplied the spoken words that persuaded the country to move bravely ahead. Appearing before the Second Continental Congress, Adams spoke with eloquence and conviction. One delegate described him as "the Atlas of American Independence." Adams's "power of thought and expression," Jefferson wrote, "moved us from our seats."

After the widespread enthusiasm that greeted the Declaration of Independence, a sense of gloom began to spread through the northern colonies. The smallpox epidemic worsened, leaving citizens and soldiers weak and in a panic searching for inoculation. Abigail nursed her own as well as neighbors' children. Even more distressing was the news of defeats suffered by American soldiers on Long Island, the capture of New York, and members of Congress fleeing Philadelphia. About twenty thousand British troops and Hessian auxiliaries were landing on American shores. But in the fall of 1777, America took hope with the first victory at Saratoga and the dramatic surrender of General Burgoyne's army. More encouraging was to hear that the retreating Gen. George Washington surprised everyone when he crossed the Delaware under darkness to seize a sleepy Hessian garrison. Days later he again struck at night, having quietly rowed back across the river, after leaving his campfires burning, to drive back British troops in New Jersey.

THE PURITAN DIPLOMAT IN PARIS

In the winter of 1777 to 1778, Adams agreed to join Arthur Lee and Ben Franklin on a commission to the Court of France to negotiate an alliance and seek financial aid. The voyage of three thousand miles took two months. It was also deadly dangerous. The north Atlantic crossing was treacherous at that time of year, and the ship could be captured by the British navy; Adams, as a leading rebel, could be tried for high treason and locked up in the Tower of London to await hanging. Abigail decided against going out of fear both parents might be captured, but she wanted their ten-year-old son Johnny to accompany his father. The boy (the future president John Quincy Adams) was eager to venture out into the seas and Abigail felt that his going out into the world was the best way to improve his understanding and sense of responsibility. Because of the many spies prowling around Boston, Adams and his son embarked secretly from Marblehead. British cruisers closed in on the American vessel, which outdistanced them due to the superior sailing skills of its captain. In the southern course a violent tropical storm hit the ship and shattered the mainmast. In his diary Adams wrote of "the ship, her motions, rollings, wringings, and agonies" and of the "devastation and purtrefaction" belowdecks.

John Adams always acknowledged his deep desire for recognition, and he would have had the chance to fulfill it in France had he not been so honest. *"Le fameux Adams?"* he was asked, leaving him wondering whether the French had in mind not him but his cousin Samuel, the notorious activist who joined artisans, riggers, and mechanics, the incendiary who gave the signal for the Boston Tea Party, the spark of the American Revolution. The French thought Adams too modest to accept the accolade, *"C'est un homme célèbre."* They also thought him the author of *Common Sense*, reprinted in France with the author's name dropped and all hostile references to monarchy dropped as well. In his diary, Adams recorded that the more he denied such popular fame, the more it eluded him, until finally, after his mission to France was assumed by Franklin, he felt "a man of whom nobody had ever heard before,—a perfect cipher; a man who does not understand a word of French; awkward in his figure, awkward in his dress; no abilities; a perfect bigot and fanatic."

At first Adams enjoyed the attention of French nobles and countesses; he particularly valued meeting Madame la Marquise de Lafayette, whose husband was in America fighting alongside Washington, and dining with the great philosopher Condorcet and the financier Baron Turgot—thinkers with whom he would later clash over the proper framework of constitutional government. But when Adams met other commissioners, he sensed trouble. One lived lavishly in Paris at America's expense; another brought his wife and children there with no intention of reporting to his post in Italy as minister to the Grand Duke of Tuscany. Neither kept bills or records made for the purchase of weapons to be shipped to America. The more frugal Adams chose to move in with Ben Franklin at Passy, located modestly on the outskirts of the city.

It was not the first time that Adams shared quarters with Franklin. Years earlier they slept in the same room, and when Adams closed the windows tight before turning in, he would awake shivering to find that Franklin had opened them wide and, instead of allowing Adams to get back to sleep, Franklin would give him a lecture on the virtues of fresh air. Later when Franklin passed away, in 1790 at the age of eighty-four, Adams told Abigail that too much open air did him in.

Not only different sleeping habits separated the two. To onlooking Parisians, the two American statesmen seemed like the anxious Puritan exasperated by the ageless playboy. At seventy, the affable Franklin was thirty years older than the stern Adams, and the old man seemed to want to prove that sensuality is not the vice of the young alone. In his diary Adams grumbled about Franklin's life of "continual dissipation," which kept him in the company of *les demi mondaines.* Franklin would come home in the wee hours of the morning and was rarely up at breakfast to discuss the business of the day. Franklin's many erotic involvements, perhaps exaggerated, became the talk of Paris. Franklin, the darling of French society, was the most famous American in Europe. People lined the streets when his carriage went by. With his coonskin cap, easy manners, scientific achievements, wise aphorisms, and clever puns, he stood as the image of the new America. Adams did not resent Franklin's popularity or his libido, but the swirl of soirées seemed frivolous in view of the needs of revolutionary America.

In Paris Adams became his most irritable self, suspecting Franklin and others of plotting against him so they could take credit for winning a peace treaty. Adams thought France intended to keep America weak and dependent upon its ally; hence France's support of restitution for the American Loyalists was far from a gesture of justice by a monarchist regime but designed to complicate things and prolong the war. Distrusting by nature, Adams faced a diplomacy of distrust. "No good diplomat in the eighteenth century would have suspended his suspiciousness," wrote the historian James H. Hutson of the Treaty of 1783. Adams, less interested than Franklin in parties and more concerned about policies, had to work with the French diplomat Count de Vergennes, whose vague utterances and indirections only made Adams wonder what America could expect from France. Vergennes sought to deal secretly and supply America with aid unbeknownst to England, lest Parliament reconcile with the colonies and join America in driving France out of the New World. Moreover, Adams and Franklin were blind to what Vergennes knew and kept to himself—that some of the secretaries serving American commissioners were British spies. Vergennes was quite comfortable with secret diplomacy and its intrigues. Compared to the more amiable Franklin, Vergennes found Adams stubborn and impatient and tried to have him recalled to America. Monarchist France had little sympathy for the cause of republican liberty in America.

Although Adams sought financial assistance, he had no desire to see America become an instrument of French diplomatic and military aims. While he requested that France send as much of her fleet as possible to America's coastal waters to cut off British supplies, he resisted any suggestion that French soldiers be allowed to fight on American soil. Nor would he accept a peace treaty with England unless accompanied by full recognition of American independence. England's overriding interest was to bring the war to an end, and thereby retain Canada; France's priority was to prolong it, thereby gaining revenge for its loss to England in the earlier French and Indian War, and to see England prostrated and forfeiting all its possessions in the New World. Adams courted England with the possibility of a postwar commercial treaty, knowing full well that a reunion of America and England was the last thing the French wished to see.

Vergennes preferred to deal with the more cooperative Franklin than the insistent Adams. English envoys in Paris, together with the Spanish ambassador, French diplomats, and American commissioners, thrashed out such issues as territorial claims to the Mississippi, fishing rights off of Newfoundland and Nova Scotia, the stability of American currency in view of debts, and the status of the Tories and the confiscation of their property. Adams insisted that the subject of the Loyalists was solely an American matter, and, since their properties had been confiscated by different states, Congress had no jurisdiction. Loyalists, Adams advised, would find life so unfriendly in postrevolutionary America, it would be better for them to remain in Canada and England.

In the summer of 1779, Adams returned to America and reported to Congress on the issues that remained to be negotiated. He also drafted a new constitution for Massachusetts, which was prefaced with a declaration of rights and prescribed the separation of power and a bicameral legislature. When Adams returned to Europe, he was appointed by Congress as minister plenipotentiary to negotiate the peace treaty. Even more than France, affluent Holland was where money could be had, and Adams departed for the Hague in October 1780, carrying with him instructions to negotiate a treaty of amity and commerce with the provinces of the Low Countries. The Dutch, though prosperous, had been unable to protect their merchant vessels from the English navy, and Adams had less trouble than he encountered in France in forming friendly connections with Amsterdam brokers and presenting America's case. Dutch writers and intellectuals drew parallels between the revolt of the Low Countries and the revolt of the American colonies. For two years Adams remained in Holland, at times growing discouraged by the reluctance of the Dutch to commit to America. But in late November 1781 came the "glorious news" of the surrender of Lord Cornwallis, the general of the English army in America, and soon a treaty of commerce was established and loans totaling 5,000,000 guilders were extended from prestigious financial houses. Upon his return to Paris, Adams was hailed for his accomplishments in Holland. Adams would regard the obtaining of loans and diplomatic recognition as the greatest political achievement of his life. To a friend he wrote: "The standard of the United States waves and flies at the Hague in triumph over . . . insolence and British pride." Then the sin-struck Adams felt his ascension. "When I go to heaven," he added, not bothering with an *if,* "I should look down over the battlements with pleasure upon the Stripes and Stars wantoning in the wind at the Hague."

Its forces routed in America, England had no choice but to negotiate a peace settlement. Now the maneuvering began. Count de Vergennes claimed that America had already won its freedom from England and thus it was irrational to believe that independence should come ahead of the treaty itself. An effect, independence, cannot precede its cause, the treaty, reasoned the French diplomat. Strangely enough, the American Congress agreed with the French that a peace treaty need not stipulate acknowledgment of America's independence. Dumbfounded, the outraged Adams threatened to resign and return home. Fortunately, Adams had the support of Franklin and the newly arrived diplomat John Jay. The three decided to ignore Congress and Vergennes and deal with the British on their own terms, making a separate treaty independently of France. Formal discussions began in the winter of 1782 and continued until the following fall. In the Treaty of Paris of 1783, it was declared: "His Britanic Majesty acknowledges the said United States . . . to be free, sovereign, and independent states." The three American diplomats held their ground, insisting upon coastal fishing rights and conceding to Europe no territorial claims in America and to the Loyalists no compensation for property. The treaty was signed in a building that is presently part of the University of the Sorbonne, in the fashionable sixth arrondissement at 56, rue de Jacob.

Adams had experienced politics at the local level in Massachusetts, but diplomacy in Europe seemed an entirely different proposition, and from his reflections one can understand why later he would, when thinking about constitutional systems, put more trust in institutions than in men "I will venture to say," he wrote in his diary,

> however feebly I may have acted my part, or whatever mistakes I may have committed, yet the situations I have been in, between angry nations and more angry factions, have been some of the most singular and interesting that ever happened to any man. The fury of enemies as well as of elements, the subtlety and arrogance of allies and, what has been worse than all, the jealousy, envy, and little pranks of friends and copatriots, would be one of the most instructive lessons in morals and politics that was ever committed to paper.

Adams may have lost his patience with compatriots as well as enemies. But with the help of Franklin and Jay, Adams accomplished something unique in U.S. history. What the Treaty of 1783 commemorated was not to be repeated in the twentieth century: America won both the war *and* the peace.

LEAVING PARIS WITH *TRISTESSE*

Adams's last days in Paris were treasured for personal as well as political reasons. While the negotiations with England had been under way, Abigail, now thirty-nine, and daughter Abigail, nicknamed Nabby, had boarded ship to sail the Atlantic and rejoin the rest of the family. On a previous brief trip back to America, John returned with his son Charles, who, though at first fearful of the high seas, turned out to be as "stout a sailor" as his older brother John Quincy, who would make numerous trips across the Atlantic serving as an American diplomat.

But the vessel on which mother and daughter sailed reeked with whale oil and vomit, and in a storm off the Grand Banks bottles and plates crashed to the floor as passengers held fast to whatever was lashed down. Women on board had to put up with two cramped, airless cabins, while the larger number of men slept in a room that served as the mess hall. The dampness of the quarters affected Abigail's rheumatism, and the meals were so revolting that often she would pitch in to prepare something more edible. When the weather improved, she left her quarters and began to "make a bustle," as she put it, describing how she "soon exerted my authority with scrapers, mops, brushes, infusions of vinegar, etc. and in a few hours you would have thought you were on a different ship."

Abigail started out terrified of the ocean, but during the crossing she sensed a certain sublimity watching the mysterious phosphorescence of the water at night. She wrote to her sister ecstatically of the "blazing ocean," as dangerous as it was divine. "Great and marvelous are Thy works, Lord God Almighty."

Mother and daughter landed in England and spent a few days in London where Adams, arriving from Holland, joined them before they crossed the channel to Calais and continued through the French countryside in a coach driven by six horses. Abigail and Nabby felt caught up in scenes from a Laurence Sterne narrative.

Adams was delighted to resettle in Paris, particularly in a spacious house with a garden located near the Bois de Boulogne. But at first Abigail and Nabby found Paris repugnant. At a loss with the language, they suspected coachmen and servants of trying to cheat them. French society seemed too leisurely and hedonistic, French women shameless in their flirtations and risqué affairs, and even priests more promiscuous than pious. But the new environment grew on them, and Adams pointed out the delights of the city: the elegant gardens; broad, tree-lined boulevards; magnificent museums; and opera and theater. Abigail became fascinated by the exquisite poise and pace of French ballerinas, and Adams recalled years earlier sitting at the opera in a box next to the famous old philosopher Voltaire. When Adams was relocated to London in 1785, Abigail spoke the sentiments of the family when she wrote in a letter to Jefferson: "I think I have somewhere met with the observation that nobody ever leaves Paris but with a degree of *tristesse*."

2

"The Most Insignificant Office
That Ever Man Contrived"

"NO ATTACHMENT BUT TO MY OWN COUNTRY"

The first duty awaiting Adams as minister to the Court of St. James was his formal presentation to the royal sovereignty. American Loyalists in England spread rumors that Adams would never be received by His Majesty. Notified otherwise, Adams hurriedly prepared a short speech promising friendly relations toward England. He bought a new coat while Abigail took out of storage his royal best: buckled shoes, silk breeches, white gloves, sash, sword, and wig. It was a strange confrontation. "Mad" King George III, known for his febrile tantrums yet the ruler of the most powerful country in the world, meets prudent John Adams, modest lawyer from the provinces yet the author of a book explaining why monarchy had no future in the coming world.

Both the king and the minister were apprehensive. Adams bowed several times and the king spoke with a tremor, inquiring of the diplomat's English ancestry, which Adams minimized, pointing out his people had left the old country more than a century and a half before. The king then suggested that Adams had become attached to France. "I must avow to Your Majesty," Adams answered, "I have no attachment but to my own country." "An honest man will never have any other," George III responded.

Although Adams hit it off with the king and found him a stimulating conversationalist, his political relations with English officials grew strained. He failed to obtain assurances that England would respect America's fishing and navigation rights, withdraw its remaining troops from America, and possibly extend commercial privileges. England's government and its people had yet to forgive America for rejecting the mother country. Then too Adams was in the awkward position of raising the question of compensation for slaves and property carried off by British officers and, at the same time, having to face the embarrassment of Americans refusing to pay debts to London creditors. To the British, never reconciled to the colonies' triumph, the American Revolution amounted to sedition and treason, a quest for license in the name of liberty. Unlike in France and Holland, Adams found the situation in England hopeless.

The one consolation was personal. Adams's daughter Nabby had married an American military officer, and a baby was on the way. Abigail found herself absorbed in gardening and once again enjoying the company of Jefferson, a lonely widower in need of female companionship. Abigail and Jefferson had already enjoyed their time together in Paris, and although Jefferson could have sharp differences with John Adams, he tenderly opened up his deepest feelings to Abigail. But Jefferson had been called to London on serious business.

The "Barbary Pirates" had seized two American ships in the Mediterranean and forced twenty-one sailors into slave labor. Most European countries had been willing to pay Tripoli, Tunisia, Algiers, and Morocco protection fees, and Congress instructed Adams and Jefferson to negotiate. An envoy of one of the sultans warned Adams that a war between Muslim and Christian would be too horrible to contemplate. Adams wondered whether he was dealing with an astute politician or a shrewd con man. He and Jefferson followed instructions and coughed up a small payment, "a drop in the bucket." The episode was American history's first lesson on why the country needed what Adams thought it did and Jefferson did not—a well-armed navy.

America needed something else that Adams thought it did and Jefferson did not—a new system of government. Prior to the peace treaty of 1783, America formally adopted the Articles of Confederation, a loose association of independent states in a nation that had no president or national court system. The period of the Confederation

represented the ultimate in decentralization, with sovereign authority located in the states rather than in the national government, and
with each state enjoying the right to enter its own commercial
treaties and deal diplomatically with foreign powers and to issue its
own currency. The Articles of Confederation presented the danger
that a European power could play the American states off one
another. It also allowed the possibility that state legislatures could
be taken over by democratic majorities and people in debt would
call for printing new currency to pay off obligations in worthless
paper. The "day of the debtors" did happen in North Carolina,
Rhode Island, and Massachusetts, as people closed down the courts
and demanded a repudiation of all debts.

Adams had been following these developments with apprehension, while Jefferson was pleased that people would take power
into their own hands. When the uprising of Daniel Shays occurred
in western Massachusetts in 1786, Jefferson felt that those who
took up arms to stop foreclosures of their farms were expressing
the honored tradition of resistance to government. "It will often be
expressed when wrong, but better so than not to be exercised at
all," he wrote to Abigail. "I like a little rebellion now and then. It is
like a storm in the Atmosphere." To Col. William Smith, Nabby's
husband and Adams's son-in-law, Jefferson was even more emphatic.
"The tree of liberty must be refreshed from time to time, with the
blood of patriots and tyrants. It is its natural manure." But John
Adams saw things differently. "Is it not an insult to common sense,
for a people with the same breath to cry *liberty*, an *abolition of debts*,
and a *division of goods?*" Adams also grasped what eluded Jefferson:
the more insurrection at the local level, the more the central government will strengthen its authority, as indeed it did with the
adoption of the new Constitution drafted at the Philadelphia convention in the fall and winter of 1787 to 1788.

In London Adams had been working on a massive treatise in
political philosophy. The three-volume text was written in part in
response to the disturbances in America but even more so in response to European criticisms of the state constitutions and of the
new federal constitution. The publication of the volumes received
some favorable attention, but when Adams returned to America

and reentered political life, that work, and a subsequent text published in 1790, became controversial. Only one other American president, Woodrow Wilson, wrote a full text on political philosophy before his election to the highest office of the land. Wilson sought to explain why a committee-run congressional government had become too cumbersome in contemporary America. Adams sought to explain why republican government had consistently failed in Europe and why it had a chance of succeeding in America, provided America ceased listening to the *philosophes*, the French thinkers who believed that reason and virtue would eliminate power and corruption. Adams's works would be the center of the storm surrounding his political career as he became vice president in 1789.

In March 1788, Adams left England to return to America after an absence of ten years. The Adams family departed convinced that their stay in Europe made them more attached to America. They did take with them a few pieces of fine furniture purchased in Paris, a load of books, and a dozen pair of silk stockings given to Abigail by Jefferson.

At sea Adams paced the deck of the *Lucretia*, bracing against the windy salt air and wondering what America would be like. What Adams did not know was that the ship had been spotted by a lighthouse off the Massachusetts shore and a cannon announced its arrival to signal a glorious welcome by the citizens of Boston. Adams was hailed as a hero of the Revolution, the diplomat who secured the timely loan from Holland and negotiated a peace treaty that made America an independent state. Upon arriving, the Adamses were escorted to a reception at the splendid Beacon Hill home of John Hancock.

Immediately speculation circulated about Adams's political future. The Constitution had been ratified, and the states selected "electors" to choose the president and vice president. No one doubted that the first office would go to Washington and that Adams would be next in line. Alexander Hamilton, however, perhaps seeing himself as the successor to Washington, or perhaps not wishing to see Adams as a close rival to his hero, worked behind the scenes to convince politicians to withhold votes from Adams. Hamilton knew that Adams would be elected but sought to keep his vote to a minimun lest the New Englander continue to be regarded as a popular hero. Hamilton succeeded. Washington won unanimously with sixty-nine votes, but Adams received only thirty-four, which put him ahead of others for second place but deeply hurt his pride. Adams knew nothing of Hamilton's politicking, but he could not help but wonder. "Is this justice?" he asked Benjamin Rush. "Is there common sense of decency in this business? Is it not an indelible stain on our country, countrymen, and constitution? I assure you I think so." Adams was so depressed he almost turned down the vice presidency.

The vote hardly reflected the esteem in which Adams was held. He was hailed in the New England press as "the great Adams," and when he entered Boston, church bells rang and crowds in the street cheered and waved their hats at him. When he left Braintree for the capital in Philadelphia, on April 13, 1789, he had a military escort, fine horses with riders fully equipped, and Adams riding in a front coach followed by a procession of forty glittering carriages.

Adams found the office of vice president less challenging than boring. Possessed of a fiery mind that had argued the case for independence, he was now asked to preside quietly in the Senate, where he was not to deliver formal addresses or even vote unless its members deadlocked in a tie. Adams was hardly used to restraining himself. His office, he told a friend, was laborious and routine, and he felt "stupidly pinched and betrayed" by representatives from New England who rarely sought his advice. At times he wished he was back practicing law where he could be active rather than passive. "My own situation is almost the only one in the world in which firmness and patience are useless." Adams was the first to occupy a position, he lamented to Abigail, that was "the most insignificant office that ever the Invention of Man contrived or his Imagination conceived."

Adams recorded no opinion on Washington's cabinet. The minor appointments were the Virginian Edmund Randolph as attorney general and the Massachusettsian Henry Knox as secretary of war.

More important were Hamilton as secretary of Treasury and Jefferson as secretary of state. In the first years of his vice presidency, Adams had no quarrels with either Hamilton or Jefferson, who treated him with courtesy and respect. But the country divided between Hamilton and Jefferson over economic policy and the moral future of the American republic.

HAMILTONIANISM, JEFFERSONIANISM, CONSTITUTIONALISM

Born in the Caribbean, Hamilton grew up with no specific identity to state or region, and he was one of the first exponents of American nationalism. Having worked as a youngster on the island of St. Kitts, buying and selling cargoes at the age of twelve, and dealing in trade and credit, Hamilton would become the genius of a budding American economy. He was the era's one thinker who recognized that government must have the power to control monetary policy, regulate commerce, and use the national debt as investment capital for the country's future. He could not help but conclude that America's destiny depends on rapid economic development and the promotion of manufacturing and industrialization. Specifically, he proposed a national bank and the federal government funding the debts the states had incurred during the Revolution. The bank proposal and especially the funding scheme created a storm of controversy. The funding seemed to benefit those who had purchased state bonds at low costs and now stood to benefit from the appreciation, and it also worked to the advantage of the most indebted states at the expense of those that made an effort at meeting their obligations. The Virginians Jefferson and Madison denounced the idea of a national bank, claiming that the Constitution never gave the government the power to create such an institution. They also saw the funding proposal as a plot, the first step toward allowing the moneyed few to ascend over the democratic many, just as in England the public debt, banknotes, and other currencies that had nothing to do with labor or land had corrupted Parliament.

In these controversies, Adams shared Hamilton's position that America could not defer paying its debts to France and Holland, lest its credit be jeopardized in other European countries. He also supported the bank, though later he would have second thoughts about the "mania for money" overtaking America. The economic issues divided the country geographically, but a compromise was reached when the South accepted Hamilton's program in exchange for having the capital moved from Philadelphia to the Potomac region.

The Federalist economic policies urged by Hamilton and supported by Adams envisioned a young republic rising dramatically to become a world power. Upon his return from Europe, Adams saw a country on the move, with the building of shipyards and canals, a rise in demand for American agricultural products, and a skilled workforce of printers, bakers, blacksmiths, gunsmiths, carpenters, instrument specialists, metal shapers, and artisan cabinetmakers. But the bank and American commerce in general were regarded with suspicion by Jefferson, who thought that Hamilton as Treasury secretary was turning the country over to "stock jobbers and king jobbers" and making America a replica of the British government. A sudden financial crisis in April 1792, which some thought had been triggered by "the rage of speculation," ruined several prominent families and increased further opposition to Hamilton's policies.

At the time, and in the writing of American history since, America's political culture has been thought to be not a little schizoid, divided as it was by Jeffersonianism and Hamiltonianism. It was seen in that light by President Washington, who would take Jefferson by the arm and try to talk him into reaching a meeting of minds with Hamilton. It was not to be. These two headstrong minds had diametrically opposed visions for America. Jefferson saw every step away from village life as a step away from virtue and down the slippery slope of vice. Hamilton rejected rural society as repressive, the environment not of liberty but of slavery. The differences between the two hardly breaks down into a radical "Left" and a conservative "Right" position. Although Jefferson liked the possibility of a "little rebellion now and then," he saw property as a stabilizing force, and he would have dreaded a true class revolution that brought about the social transformation of the existing order. Hamilton would introduce industry and commerce, a truly disrupting force, and he looked not to property but to the circulation of money and credit as liberating America from the inertia of rural life.

Adams could be at ease with neither Jeffersonianism nor Hamiltonianism. He hardly believed that differences in geography or economy would affect character and conduct, as though the *human heart* (one of his favorite terms) changes if it leaves the Virginian farm to take up residence in the merchant offices of New York City. Adams believed that the nature of humankind remained relatively unchanged regardless of circumstances. "The world has been too long abused with the notion," he warned, that soil, climate, and the mode of the economy "decides the character and political institutions of nations." On the contrary, it was precisely the nature and structure of government and its institutions that decides a nation's character and its historical fate. America could flourish on the farm or in the banking system, but if the Constitution is ill devised, the country will go the way of all other failed republics. Adams may be described as a political determinist who put his trust in institutions. Neither the elite classes nor the democratic masses would be the salvation of the nation. It would be mechanisms of government guided by the directive imagination of a responsible president.

Of the three leading thinkers of the era, it could be said that Hamilton was a mercantilist who believed in the fusion of state and economy, Jefferson an individualist who believed in the sovereignty of the people, Adams a constitutionalist who believed in the efficacy of government. Hamilton looked to the oligarchical few who would be motivated by responsibility, Jefferson to the democratic many who would guard their freedom with jealousy, Adams to the single executive who would preserve liberty by relying upon government and its "machinery."

There was no possible reconciliation between Jefferson and Hamilton, each of whom feared the ascendancy of the other. The only matter they could agree upon was that Washington was indispensable and must remain in office for a second term. What of Adams?

THE VICE PRESIDENT AND THE "GLARE OF ROYALTY"

More than Hamilton's economic policies, it was the French Revolution that divided America down the middle. Adams had already written a book addressed to French political philosophers, and when the revolution broke out he wrote another that had Americans perplexed as to how he stood, or, to use modern parlance, where he was coming from. Jefferson had no doubt that Adams was a closet monarchist, and when Thomas Paine published his *Rights of Man* in London, in spring of 1791, Jefferson wrote a letter and sent it along with his copy of the book to a Philadelphia printer. The letter, appearing as a preface, encouraged Americans to read Paine's book as an answer "to the political heresies which had of late sprung up among us." Few readers doubted that Jefferson had Adams in mind, the "Duke of Braintree," as an anti-Federalist editor had dubbed him, so convinced was he that the vice president was trying to introduce the principles of aristocracy and even monarchy into American political life. In writing against the French Revolution, Adams came to be seen as a reactionary trying to uphold the old order. Actually, Adams was a liberal warning the French that unless they followed his advice, their revolution would go off course and end in disaster.

His critics, however, saw the French Revolution as the natural extension of the principles of the American Revolution, and they charged Adams with hypocrisy for having advocated one revolution and not the other. The British philosopher Edmund Burke had also defended the American Revolution and become a discerning critic of the French. But Adams's critique of the faulty thinking of the French had been published before the revolution broke out in 1789, whereas Burke's *Reflections on the Revolution in France* appeared in 1791. Adams's writings on political philosophy will be dealt with in our next chapter. Here one might note that to some extent Adams brought on such reactionary accusations against himself by his own conduct in stepping into the office of vice president.

The first few days Adams served as vice president he was tense and nervous, uncertain how his office should be conceived and how he should conduct himself. The Constitution made him president of the Senate but without specifying any codes of protocol. Adams wondered how the president should be addressed when he entered the halls of Congress, and he proposed that the Speaker of the House be prefaced with the accolade "Honorable." Much discussion ensued about titles and rituals, and a committee suggested greeting President Washington with "His Highness." Adams asked the Senate: "Whether I should say, 'Mr. Washington,' 'Mr. President,' 'Sir,' 'may it please your Excellency,' or what else? I observed that it had been common while he commanded the army to call him 'His Excellency,' but I was free to own it would appear to me better to give him no title but 'Sir' or 'Mr. President,' than to put him on a level with a governor of Bermuda."

From his time in Europe Adams had watched Parliament and the Court behave with regal address and ritual bows, and he became convinced that America could use a touch of dignity and decorum in the affairs of government. But Adams was no longer in Europe, and back in America he seemed a fop on a fool's errand.

His antagonists came at him as though America's masculine identity was at stake. William Maclay was a rough, no-frills, hard-hitting lawyer and senator from Pennsylvania. Before the press and Congress he ridiculed the vice president's "silly" and "vain" fetish for pompous titles and ceremonies. Adams fought back, lecturing the Senate on the importance of deference, respect, and etiquette. Maclay sneered at Adams's "trivial distinctions" and his "wretched" quest for the splendor of royalty. Adams's "pride, obstinacy and folly are equal to his vanity," said Maclay, who warned Americans that a "court party" was forming in the country, invoking memories of the corrupt corridors of power surrounding royalty in Europe. The historian Charles Beard described Maclay as "the original Jeffersonian Democrat."

The phrase "kingly authority" came to be associated with Adams, and the impression grew that he had returned from England an ardent admirer of the monarchy and court prerogatives. In his running notebook, Jefferson described his impressions of Adams:

> Mr. Adams had originally been a republican. The glare of royalty and nobility during his mission to England, had made

him believe their fascination a necessary ingredient in government; and Shays' rebellion, not sufficiently understood where he then was, seemed to prove that the absence of want and oppression, was not a sufficient guarantee of order. His book on the American constitutions having made known his political bias, he was taken up by the monarchial federalists in his absence, and on his return to the United States, he was made to believe that the general disposition of our citizens was favorable to monarchy. He here wrote his 'Davila,' as a supplement to the former work, and his election to the Presidency confirmed him in his errors. Innumerable addresses too, artfully and industriously poured in upon him, deceived him into a confidence that he was on the pinnacle of popularity, when the gulf was yawning at his feet, which was to swallow up him and his deceivers. For when General Washington was withdrawn, these *energumeni* [fanatics] of royalism, kept in check hitherto by the dread of his honesty, his firmness, his patriotism, and the authority of his name, now mounted on the car of State and free from control, like Phaeton on that of the sun, drove headlong and wild, looking neither right nor left, nor regarding anything but the objects they were driving at; until, displaying these fully, the eyes of the nation were opened, and a general disbandment of them from the public councils took place.

This long passage needs to be pondered not only to hear Jefferson thinking for himself. More important, it is, in American political history, the first utterance of a reverse "Red Scare." In the twentieth century, America witnessed several episodes when the American people had the impression that some diplomats or intellectuals were the ideological agents of a foreign revolutionary power. In the telling passage above, Jefferson did offer one profound insight: Adams and the Federalist Party need not have feared Shays's Rebellion, for in a country without "want and oppression" there is not going to be a revolution. But Jefferson was worried about something else. If Adams and his party stayed in power, there was certain to be a counterrevolution. Even worse, since America never had on native grounds an aristocracy and monarchy to overthrow in 1776, two decades later the *energumeni* were trying to sneak such institutions into the country. Adams saw himself serving the cause of republicanism; Jefferson depicted him as subverting it. Was he?

THE BATHOS OF OPPOSITION POLITICS

It is doubtful that any of Adams's critics had read his political writings of the period 1788–1790, although the Virginian John Taylor would do so in later years, leading to a stimulating exchange of letters between the two. Most likely Jefferson never read them either, for he did not bother to quote from them. Adams's political writings were actually read more in France than in America in the period following the revolution of 1789, when a minority of French thinkers, called the *anglomanes*, desired to be guided by Adams and looked to British political institutions as models. Even though Adams assured Jefferson, time and time again, that he had no intention of bringing aristocracy and monarchy to America, Jefferson refused to believe him, whether for political reasons or out of a genuine conviction that Adams harbored dangerous thoughts. Indeed, Jefferson suggests that the "glare" of such royal institutions had so blinded Adams that he was importing them whether he was aware of it or not. Whatever his subjective intent, Adams was objectively a victim of guilt by affection, too much enamored of un-American ideas and institutions. Adams may only have been misguided, but he was a menace nevertheless. And when Jefferson said that finally the "eyes of the nation were opened" and a "general disbandment" of Adams and the Federalist Party took place, he strongly implied that America turned toward him, the true heir to George Washington and the real savior of the country.

Actually the election of 1800 was, as we shall see, quite close, and if Jefferson implied that Adams and the old Federalist Party represented a threat to America, it is curious that the new Republican Party adopted most of its policies. It is even more curious that Jefferson depicts Adams, who stood for nothing if not systematic discipline, as wildly riding the legendary Roman coach Phaeton and careening out of control. And the American people, supposedly antimonarchical all along, had to be awakened from their own spell once they became aware of the "objects" Adams and his party "were driving at." Since Jefferson and his party ended up not so much repudiating the opposition party as appropriating its place, what were the objects they were driving at?

The question is vital, for the origins of American politics around the institution of the presidency came into being at this moment in American history. Jefferson's comments are revealing. Depicting Adams as a monarchist, Jefferson sees himself as stepping forth to rid the country of subversive elements. What goes unmentioned is the object of his own ambitions. He aspires to the presidency as much as Adams as vice president expects it. The battle for the presidency was born of like for like, two rivals vying for the same object, and it was expedient for the opposition to create a sense of difference to conceal the power struggle. Once victory is won, the differences can be denied, as indeed Jefferson does deny them in his inaugural address when he reassures Americans: "We are all Republicans, we are all Federalists." It is in the nature of American politics to create the appearance of conflict only better to affirm the reality of consensus.

Party politics in America begins in bravado and ends in bathos, an electoral campaign that promises a climactic resolution and succumbs to the ordinary trivia of everyday politics. When the election is over, the enemy other becomes the friendly we, and what appeared to be a real struggle of opposing forces turns out to be a charade. Adams and the Federalists, it should be noted, were just as responsible as Jefferson and the Republicans for setting American politics off on a false note. For if the Republicans saw unanimity and harmony everywhere, the Federalists could see nothing but diversity and conflict. Not until Alexis de Tocqueville came to the United States in the 1830s, and wrote *Democracy in America*, did one become aware that both factions started out with erroneous assumptions. The Republicans scarcely thought that uncontrolled democracy could lead to the "tyranny of the majority," and the Federalists never understood that their idea of a "mixed" government of checks and balances had no chance of working had America not enjoyed a political culture of homogeneity. Jefferson believed that the people would be virtuous if left unmolested by government, while Adams believed that the "machinery of government" was necessary to make people virtuous. Both assumed that the future of freedom depended upon either the will of the people or the workings of government. But half a century later Tocqueville would observe: "Americans are not virtuous, yet they are free." Tocqueville told Americans what both Jefferson and Adams failed to grasp: A country that had skipped the feudal stage of history and had neither a proletariat nor an aristocracy, neither those who would forge a revolution nor those who would resist it, such a unique country need not worry about the restoration of monarchy or the assault on property. Both Jefferson and Adams saw conflict: with the former it was the many against the few, and with the latter the few against the many; that is, on the one side democracy and its desires and on the other property and its possessions. What explained America, Tocqueville pointed out, was not conflict but consensus, the values of property, opportunity, and natural rights that all Americans shared in common. Democracy would pose no threat to property, as Adams feared, and property would no longer be the inherited privilege of aristocracy, as Jefferson feared. It took a European to come to America to tell America to cease looking to Europe and recognize that America is exceptional in having escaped the class fears of the Old World.

As a political philosophy, Jeffersonianism had much to offer America by way of liberty and the doctrine of natural rights. As a political phenomenon involving electoral politics, however, Jeffersonianism was born in frustration and propelled by ambition. The Virginians, we should remember, saw themselves as the real founders, having led America through its trying revolutionary years. Patrick Henry was among the first to thunder against the Stamp Act, Peyton Randolph led the Continental Congress, Washington commanded the army, and Jefferson wrote the Declaration of Independence. The possible election of Adams to the presidency would deny Virginia its role as the country's vanguard.

Recent research has demonstrated that Jefferson furtively organized opposition to Adams by spreading scandalous rumors and hiring journalists to find dirt, even though he denied such activity at the time; in later years, in his long correspondence with the former vice president, he again reassured Adams, and Abigail, that he was not behind the skullduggery. Actually, the partisan campaign began earlier in the Washington administration, when Jefferson and Madison became convinced that the great general had allowed himself to be misused by Hamilton and Adams, whose policies of finance and national authority were supposedly undoing the principles of the Revolution. Jefferson even hired, with government money, the poet-journalist Philip Freneau to use his *National Gazette* to attack the Federalist Party as disloyal, so pro-English as to be returning the country to the curse of monarchy.

Given Jefferson's distrust of Adams, one can only wonder whether the Virginian's canting democracy served to conceal his own aristocratic temperament. His plantation environment, after all, breathed the air of the gentry leisure class. "With the development of slavery," observed the historian Edward Channing, "the southern agriculturalist became a magnate, the white race an aristocracy, and its more prosperous and stronger men a true landed oligarchy—the 'Virginia Lordlings.'"

During the election year of 1796, Jefferson wrote Adams to thank him for a book on the French Revolution. "But it is on politics," Jefferson explained, implying why he had no interest in it, "a subject I never loved and now hate." Earlier, when the French Revolution broke out and he was asked his own party loyalties, he wrote in a private letter: "If I could not go to heaven but with a party, I would not go there at all." But heaven was one thing, the presidency another, and Jefferson had no hesitation organizing a party to bring down the Adams administration. Jefferson believed in democracy, openness, the healthy clash of ideas, and he even claimed that "differences of opinion, like difference of face, are a law of nature, and should be viewed with the same tolerance." But when it came to politics, Jefferson lost his philosophical calm. Instead of tolerating differences, he dramatized them. He had supported the Federalist Constitution in 1789, but with Adams's election, he convinced himself that America would no longer be functioning as a republic and that it was his responsibility to organize forces against the administration. But instead of debating issues openly and publicly, as one who believed in democracy would, Jefferson hovered in the shadows. "PS," he added to a letter to the Virginian John Taylor, "it is hardly necessary to caution you to let nothing of mine go before the public." What the secretive Jefferson dreaded was precisely what Adams defended, the primacy of the executive office. The U.S. Constitution guaranteed "a republican form of government" to the states, but what of the national government? In the same letter where he claimed he would choose not to go to heaven with a party, he protested that there were no limits to "the perpetual reeligibility of the President."

With Adams as president, Jefferson felt a private anxiety he publicly denied. He wrote to James Madison to reassure him that he had "no feelings which would revolt at a secondary position to Mr. Adams. I am his junior in life, was his junior in Congress, his junior in the diplomatic line, his junior lately in the civil government." He told Elbridge Gerry that "the second office of this government is honarable & easy, the first is but splendid misery." Hamiltonians, he complained to Gerry in 1797, are whispering "machinations" about his ambitions. Nothing could be more alienating "to the pleasure of cordiality when we suspect that it is suspected. I cannot help thinking, that it is impossible for Mr. Adams to believe that the state of my mind is what it really is; that he may think I view him as an obstacle in my way." Within a year Jefferson would so view Adams, and years after he left office Jefferson would regard his election to the presidency as the ultimate vindication of the American Revolution. "The toryism with which we struggled in '77 differed but in name from the federalism of '99, with which we struggled also." At the time of Adams's administration, he reassured Europeans that he was fighting their battle on American soil. "It would give you a fever," he wrote to Philip Mazzei in 1796, "were I to name to you the apostates who have gone over to those heresies, men who were Samsons in the fields & Solomons in the council, but who have had their heads shorn by the harlot of England."

To be a successful president requires not only governing well but knowing who's out to get you. Did Adams? He should have. Adams wondered about what he called the "aristocratical passions" because they are subtle and suppressed, with minds thinking themselves so superior they are unwilling to face what it is that is driving them into intrigue and dishonesty. With such persons, Adams observed in his philosophical writings, "ambition strengthens at every advance, and at last takes possession of the whole soul so absolutely, that man sees nothing in the world of importance to others, or himself, but his object." Such figures constitute "a curious speculation," for proud aristocrats see themselves as "adorned with virtue, prudence, and benevolence" and refuse to acknowledge their oligarchical tendencies to organize and dominate. "The cunning with which they hide themselves from others, and from the man himself, too; the patience with which they wait for opportunities"—these and other such traits of self-deception convinced Adams that an aristocracy is not to be trusted and must be controlled. Yet Jefferson portrayed Adams himself as an aristocrat in collaboration with monarchism.

When one considers Adams's insights as a psychologist of human behavior together with his own behavior, a paradox confronts us. Although he saw so well how certain people move toward power while parading themselves as acting for the most benevolent motives, Adams turned out to be almost helpless before Jefferson and his opposition. In his writings, Adams was perfectly aware of the cunning nature of opposition politics. "It is almost the universal practice for each party to charge the leaders of the other with every base action, every sinister event, and every high-minded wickedness, without much consideration or inquiry, whether there is truth or evidence, or even color, to support the accusation." Yet Adams was surprised and deeply hurt by the aggressive tactics of the Republican opposition, and he would not stoop to such tactics himself, though his own party was not above it.

If Adams's critics were correct in their charges, the evidence would lie, as Jefferson himself insisted, in Adams's writings, which will now be closely examined. Given the accusations made about his texts, it could be said of Adams's brilliant political writings that they constitute the most misunderstood body of political thought in American history.

3

The Prescience of
the Political Mind

"MELANCHOLY REFLECTIONS"

To follow the mind of John Adams is to appreciate why a revolution cannot survive without a constitution. In a letter to James Warren, written in 1776 a few months before the Declaration of Independence, Adams expressed no surprise that many Americans were reluctant to make the break with the mother country. "All great changes are irksome to the human mind, especially those which are attended with great dangers and uncertain effects. No man living can foresee the consequences of such a measure," he warned, and he was worried not only about the outcome of the war. "We may please ourselves with the prospect of free and popular governments, but there is great danger that these governments will not make us happy. God grant they may! But I fear that in every Assembly members will obtain an influence by noise, not sense; by meanness, not greatness, by ignorance, not learning; by contracted hearts, not large souls." Shortly before writing his thoughts, Adams encountered on the road a "horse jockey," a town deadbeat, what the Marxists would later call a *lumpenproletarian*:

> He was always in the Law, and has been sued in many actions, at almost every court. As soon as he saw me, he came up to me, and his first Salutation to me was 'Oh! Mr. Adams what great things have you and your colleagues done for Us! We can never be grateful enough to you. There are no Courts of

Justice now in this Province, and I hope there never will be another!' . . . Is this the Object for which I have been contending? said I to myself, for I rode along without any answer to this Wretch. Are these the Sentiments of such a People? And how many of them are there in the Country? Half the Nation for what I know: for half the Nation are debtors if not more, and these have been in all Countries the Sentiments of Debtors. If the Power of the Country should get into such hands, and there is great danger that it will, to what purpose have we sacrificed our Time, health and every Thing else? Surely we must guard against this Spirit and these Principles or we shall repent of all our Conduct. However the good Sense and Integrity of the Majority of the great Body of the People, came into my thoughts for my relief, and the last resource was after all in a good Providence. How much reason there was for these melancholy reflections, the subsequent times have too fully shewn.

Adams went from being a revolutionary optimist to a constitutional pessimist, one who believed that liberty required controls and that the people needed to be protected, even from themselves. But Adams's Republican critics accused him of espousing forms of government that would protect only the elite classes, and hence the second president of the United States came to be regarded as less than loyal to the "spirit of '76" and the very meaning of a republic. No less than Jefferson himself insisted that evidence of Adams's aristocratic and monarchist tendencies can be found in his writings. Can they?

The first tome in question is John Adams's *A Defence of the Constitutions of the United States of America*. It had been prompted by a letter written by Anne-Robert J. Turgot to Dr. Richard Price on March 22, 1778. Years earlier Adams had dined with Turgot, former finance minister to Louis XVI. That was then; now, hearing of America's new state constitutions, Turgot fumed with impatience and bewilderment. Why the complicated mechanisms of checks and balances, divisions of power, and a bicameral legislature with upper and lower houses? All this clumsy apparatus is unnecessary,

Turgot complained, since America had neither a king, a nobility, nor a peasantry or plebeian class that would have required a proper dispersion of power. Turgot had good reason to complain, since his own efforts at reform in France were blocked by entrenched interest groups in Parliament. But he and other French critics believed that a "mixed" government mistakenly copies the antiquated English system. Turgot advocated, as had another Adams antagonist, the seventeenth-century English journalist and political philosopher Marchamont Nedham, placing authority in a single national assembly that would represent all classes, and in doing so obliterate all class distinctions.

More directly, Adams received four letters from Abbe de Mably, the French constitutional theorist, urging him to uphold everything in America that will "bring all the citizens together in peace and pleasure" and so sponsor festivals and parades in honor of the Fourth of July. Specifically, Mably was asking Adams to celebrate a consensus, a sense of unity, patriotism, respect for law, religiosity, and social solidarity, the very ingredients that neither Adams nor the framers could count upon when conceiving the Constitution.

Adams's reply to the European critics of America's political system turned out to be the three-volume *Defence*, begun in 1786 and completed two years later. Adams wrote at a rapid pace, and many readers, then and now, found the volumes impenetrable. No wonder. The text is written by an author who defers to classical writers only to distance himself from them. The tome is dense, meandering, sprawling, disconnected, without introductions or transitions, a jarring blur of free association about Western political philosophy that reads almost as a stream of consciousness composed by a night thinker in a dialogue with himself.

Yet in one respect the entire edifice of Adams's complex argument appears on the title pages in a single line from Alexander Pope:

All nature's difference keeps all nature's peace.

Amazing! Today, in America's multicultural political environment, the emphasis is on difference and diversity. The premise is that uniformity and consensus signify the domination of the powers that be. In Adams's eighteenth century, however, it was the French revolutionaries who argued for homogeneity as liberating and differences as repressive. The assumption was that a political system that represented distinct class strata in different branches of government would result in perpetuating the aristocratic rule of the old order. Adams, together with the *Federalist* authors, were the first thinkers in Western political philosophy to identify liberty not with unity but with diversity. Nature's difference will keep the peace.

The principle of diversity had not been fully appreciated in classical republican thought. Although Aristotle saw society divided into the rich, poor, and "middle sort," Adams found his theory of politics "inhumane" and "cruel" since it excluded "husbandman, merchant, and tradersman" from representation in the polis. Machiavelli was an ardent republican, but his story of liberty failed, in Adams's estimate, to discern how the nobility dominated almost every episode in Italian political life. The author of *History of Florence* assumed that the rich and educated, the *prominènti e cognoscente*, could be assimilated in a general representative body in the doge. But Adams believed social orders must be made to reside in different representative branches, kept apart lest they wage war upon one another. While democracy could be tempted to use its numerical superiority to overwhelm the rich and able, aristocracy would take advantage of its superior learning and guile to oppress the popular masses. Adams was as much concerned about the aggressiveness of an arrogant aristocracy as he was of democracy's tendency to disrupt into rage and disorder. But ultimately the liberty of the many depended upon the control of the few. Adams's defense of bicameralism and an upper house Senate in the United States was based on his hope that the American aristocrat could be relegated to that chamber, "a polite ostracism," as he put it, where the country "may still hope for the benefits of his exertions, without dreading his passions." Adams would isolate the aristocracy the better to put it under surveillance and control.

Was Adams, then, a monarchist? Nowhere in the text does he invoke the stale doctrine of the "divine right" of kings. Instead he emphasizes that "the body of the people is the sovereign source and the fountain and original of all power and authority, executive, legislative, and judicial." In the historical past a wise king would mediate between the poor and the rich, the "credulous many" and the "artful few," knowing that the latter class would take advantage of the former. Adams looked to the modern executive office to play the same role lest the superior talents in the Senate "swallow up" the less educated members of the House. The cases for absolute monarchy and an inherited aristocracy are nowhere to be found in the *Defence*, not even as a lesson. The Englishman Marchamont Nedham "proceeds to search for examples all over the world" to teach about the historical significance of "monarchy, absolute hereditary monarchy; but as Americans have no thoughts of introducing this form of government, it is none of their concern to vindicate the honour of such kings or kingdoms."

It is *Discourses on Davila*, published in 1790, just after he became vice president, that Adams's critics cited as a monarchist text. There is, indeed, a description of royalty as a sociological phenomenon that would explain why, even in our democratic era, throngs of people line the streets of London to watch the king and queen pass by. "An illustrious descent attracts the notice of mankind. A single drop of royal blood, however illegitimately scattered, will make any man or woman proud or vain. Why? Because, although it excites the indignation of the many, and the envy of more, it still attracts the *attention* of the world. Noble blood, whether, the nobility be hereditary or elected, and indeed, more in republican governments than in monarchies, least of all in despotisms, is held in estimation for the same reason." People, out of emotional need, look up to those they think deserve their respect or even curiosity or envy, and, Adams notes, as though anticipating today's *People* magazine, names and reputations are everything, and not necessarily the actual persons, whatever their character. "National gratitude descends from the father to the son, and is often stronger to the latter than to the former." It is as though Adams is our contemporary postmodernist advising us that we respond to signs and representations, not to people themselves but to their names and the sounds of their names. America may not have royalty, but it will have a Rockefeller, Adams might have said. "His name is often a greater distinction than a title, a star, a garter. It is this that makes so many men proud, and so many others envious of illustrious descent. The pride is as irrational and contemptible as the pride of riches, and no more."

Those who charged Adams with advocating monarchy refused to consider what he was actually explaining in *Discourses*. The overwhelming majority of the American people themselves, after all, remained loyal to the British monarchy until the outbreak of the Revolution, when they then redefined themselves as republican. But what Adams was saying is that the same emotions that attach to a monarchy adhere to a republic, the same impulse to emulation, envy, adulation, approbation, recognition, the same trappings of robes and jewelry, the same sounds of pomp and circumstance:

> Has there ever been a nation who understood the human heart better than The Romans, or made a better use of the passion for consideration, congratulation, and distinction? . . . *Distinctions of conditions*, as well as of ages, were made by difference of clothing. . . . The chairs of ivory; the lictors; . . . the crowns of gold, or ivory, of flowers; . . . their orations; and their triumphs; everything in religion, government and common life, was parade, representation and ceremony. Everything was addressed to the emulation of the citizens, and everything was calculated to attract the attention, to allure the consideration, and excite the congratulations of the people; to attach their hearts to individual citizens according to their merit; and to their lawgivers, magistrates, and judges, according to their rank, station and importance to the state. And this was in the true spirit of republics, in which form of government there is no consistent method of preserving order or procuring submission to the laws.

In a monarchy or in a republic, politics lives by attracting attention, whether it be by a parade or a news conference, or even by what the historian Daniel J. Boorstin has called a "pseudo-event," a forthcoming announcement by a press secretary who reports that he has nothing to report.

The French, in addition to criticizing America's new political system for its allegedly overlayed mechanisms of balance and control, cited another feature of the Constitution that had more to do with absence than prescence. "Where," the critics said, in effect, "is Virtue?" If a political regime were to exist without a monarchy, it was essential that both the people and its leaders have a capacity for civic virtue and, hence, be willing to dedicate themselves to the public good. The American architects of the Constitution demurred. While Hamilton felt that modern commerce and entrepreneurial energy could substitute for the older principle of virtue, Madison thought that the political process might "refine" and "enlarge" the views of the electorate so as to direct them to something higher than naked self-interest. But Adams's position is unique. He became convinced that not only is classical virtue unrealistic in modern times but that it never really played the role that philosophers claimed it did in the past.

In the *Defence* Adams scrutinizes all the meanings of virtue: the Roman ideals of courage and manliness, the ancient principles of prudence, justice, temperance, and fortitude, and even the Christian concept, "so much more sublime," observed Adams, of Jonathan Edwards's Calvinist ethic of "universal benevolence." Of all the concepts of virtue, the one that troubled Adams the most was Montesquieu's notion of the individual sacrificing his private interests for the sake of the public good. The idea that humankind could go against its natural inclinations and engage in what Montesquieu called "a renouncement of self" seemed preposterous to Adams. "If the absence of avarice is necessary to republican virtue, can you find any age or country in which republican virtue has existed?"

ADAMS'S CRITIQUE OF THE ENLIGHTENMENT

Adams's reflections on political philosophy represented the most probing expression of the American Enlightenment, or perhaps the

"Counter-Enlightenment" since the *Defence* posed a challenge to its European counterpart. In modern history there have been three criticisms leveled against the American Constitution and the Enlightenment that infused it. The first charge, made by the French, held that all the checks and balances were unnecessary since America escaped the social conditions of the Old World. The second indictment, made by the poets and philosophers of New England transcendentalism, complained that the Constitution, "A Machine That Would Go By Itself," was not only deadening but left no place for the activity of mind and the role of the intellectual. The third critique, made by our contemporary schools of poststructuralism and deconstruction, makes the opposite charge and claims that the Enlightenment thinkers, Adams among them, placed too much trust in reason to the neglect of the power realities that would thwart it.

At first glance, the contemporary French critics of Adams appear to have been correct in looking over to America and seeing an environment of solidarity. America did indeed turn out to be a nation of consensus, as Alexis de Tocqueville would later observe in his travels through the United States in the 1830s, returning to France convinced that America's Constitution was a "chimera" based on the fallacy of a "mixed" government in a country lacking the mixed social orders of the Old World. Adams insisted in thinking of politics as a triangular phenomenon of power, with the one (monarchy or executive), the few (aristocracy), and the many (democracy) poised against one another. The differences between Adams and Jefferson had little to do with democracy. "We agree perfectly," Adams noted to Jefferson, "that the many should have a full, fair, and perfect representation. You are apprehensive of monarchy, I of aristocracy. I would therefore give more power to the president and less to the Senate." Adams feared giving the Senate the right to approve of executive appointments, and Jefferson feared that the president would be continuously reelected or perhaps have a son inherit the office, one of the rumors leveled at John Quincy Adams. But the tripartite formula of the one, few, and many seemed a relic of the Old World. To the extent that such clear class distinctions never took root in what became a homogeneous middle-class

America, it would appear that Adams was wrong to devise schemes to control them. Were the French critics right? Only to the extent that they assumed that class systems were at the basis of social conflict. But that is far from Adams's view of reality. To appreciate the uniqueness of Adams's perspective, let us consider the views of three European thinkers.

Niccolò Machiavelli assumed, as Adams well knew in challenging the assumption, that if the Italian nobility had only been content with what it had and restrained its predatory instincts, it would have ceased being the enemy of other classes. Centuries later, Karl Marx assumed that if the working class would only be bitterly discontent with what it did not have, it could transform the world and get rid of all of its class oppressions. But America need not worry about Machiavelli or Marx, advised Tocqueville, for it had neither a restless nobility nor an aggressive working class. Machiavelli, Marx, and Tocqueville all assumed, in short, that conflict reflected the realities of class, and without the clashes of class there would be only the coherence of consensus. Why, then, should Adams have been worried about class conflict when America had no class system?

To Adams, conflict had less to do with class structures than with deep human emotions and anxieties, atavistic traits that had been the stuff of power politics throughout history. Adams agreed with Machiavelli that the impossibility of satisfying endless desires leads to irritation and antagonism. But when he came upon a passage by Machiavelli claiming that the Florentines had rid themselves of the sources of conflict, he jumped on it like a panther. "There seemed to be no seeds of future differences left in Florence," wrote Machiavelli, and Adams explodes: "No seeds! Not one had been eradicated; all the seeds that ever existed remained in full vigor. The seeds were in the human heart."

Conflict arises not simply from class phenomena but from the human soul divided against itself as a result of original sin. Adams would go to his death not at all certain about the existence of God and the afterlife, but like the modern thinkers Friedrich Nietzsche and Reinhold Niebuhr he also discerned the will to power and self-aggrandizement as inherent in the human condition. One of

Adams's first essays written as a youth was "On Self-Delusion," and he saw the human animal as a rationalizing creature who regards his intentions as a matter of conscience rather than the ego. The conflicts that arise in human affairs have less to do with class systems than with moral corruptions, less rooted in the strength of political structures than in the weakness of human character.

Adams's *Defence* examines the distortions of philosophical discourse made by thinkers like Machiavelli, who flattered the citizens of Florence rather than telling them the truth about themselves. The same was true of Jefferson, who would have Americans believe they are "the chosen people of God" and whose republican commitment confirmed his "confidence in their ultimate good sense and virtue." Adams sought to awaken Americans to the temptations that beset them as the first step in trying to overcome and control them. But in Jefferson's America, democracy yields to desire in the name of idealism. "It is this penetration into the dishonesty of rational idealism which established affinities between Nietzsche and classical Christianity," observed Niebuhr. Adams's critique of classical thought drew upon a Christian perspective, and in that dark, tragic outlook on life, conflict can no more be removed than sin can be absolved.

Adams's son John Quincy Adams lived into the age of Jacksonian democracy and the school of thought called transcendentalism, which flowered among the poets and philosophers of New England. Such writers as Ralph Waldo Emerson and Henry David Thoreau felt themselves alienated from the American Constitution that Adams senior took so much trouble to defend. Recall that the *Federalist* authors saw no clear role for intellectuals in the Constitution. Poets and philosophers not only felt excluded but wondered how a political system based on mechanisms could ever yield up morality and virtue, particularly a system based on distrust and suspicion. Adams had dealt with this matter in the conclusion of volume three of the *Defence*. "Happiness, whether in despotism or democracy, whether in slavery or liberty, can never be found without virtue," he observed in agreement with Aristotle. But he departed from philosophers and poets by suggesting that something good just may develop out of a system of controls. "The best republics will be virtuous, and have been so; but we may hazard a conjecture, that the virtues have been the effect of the well-ordered constitution, rather than the cause: and perhaps it would be impossible to prove, that a republic cannot exist, even among highwaymen, by setting one rogue to watch another; and the knaves themselves may, in time, be made honest men by the struggle."

John Adams had also addressed the third criticism of the Constitution and the philosophy of the Enlightenment. It has been held that the thinkers of the Enlightenment placed too much trust in reason and remained innocent about the power realities of the world. The assumption was, the critics charged, that eighteenth-century political philosophers look to the rise of knowledge as an answer to the riddles of power. Knowledge becomes genuine knowledge only when arrived at rationally and accepted under conditions free of coercion. Knowledge is, by definition then, the opposite of power. Did Adams subscribe to this assumption? On the contrary, Adams proves to be a very modernist thinker in his conviction that knowledge is not necessarily enlightening or redemptive. The increase of knowledge may lead to advances in science without contributing to the moral progress of the human condition. Indeed, knowledge may exacerbate human imperfections by making it possible to carry them out more effectively. "Does not the increase of knowledge in any man increase his emulation, and the diffusion of knowledge among men increase their rivalries?" The advent of knowledge hardly lessens the need for political controls. "Has the progress of sciences, arts, and letters yet discovered that there are no passions in human nature—no ambition, avarice, or desire of fame?" Jefferson and many of the French philosophers did believe that the passions would yield to reason and that scientific knowledge would contribute to the moral education of society. But Adams scours the record of the historical past to doubt that hopeful expectation:

> Had Cicero less vanity, or Caesar less ambition, for their vast Erudition? Had the King of Prussia less of one than the others? There is no connection in the mind between science and passion by which the former can extinguish or diminish the

latter. It, on the contrary, sometimes increases them by giving them exercise. Were the passions of the Romans less vivid in the age of Pompey than in the time of the Mummius? Are those of the Britons more moderate at this hour than in the reigns of the Tudors. Are the passions of monks the weaker for all their learning? Are not jealousy, envy, hatred, malice, and revenge, as well as emulation and ambition, as rancourous in the cells of the Carmelites as in the courts of princes? . . . Go to Paris—how do you find the men of letters? United, friendly, harmonious, meek, humble, modest, charitable? Prompt to mutual forbearance? Unassuming? Ready to acknowledge superior merit? Zealous to encourage the first symptoms of genius? Ask Voltaire and Rousseau, Marmontel and De Mably.

WHAT, NO DISTINCTIONS IN AMERICA!

The above passage comes from Adams's *Discourses on Davila*, written shortly before he became vice president in 1789 and published the following year. A "heavy and dull volume," as Adams called it, the text was a response to a series of reflections in a book by an Italian scholar writing on the French civil wars and uprisings of the sixteeenth century. Adams scrutinizes the commentary and concludes that its author had little understanding of what had gone on historically because he followed the classical tradition and saw humankind as a political animal and not a social creature. It is not devotion to politics that drives human nature, Adams notes in departing from Aristotle, but instead an absorption with society in all its rites and rituals. Adams takes political philosophy away from politics and relocates it in sociology and psychology, in the study of social interaction and human motivation. Society is the focus, and it is society and social order that are threatened by the French Revolution.

The specter that hovered over that revolution was Jean-Jacques Rousseau, the philosopher who abandoned his five children to an orphanage while he busied himself plotting the total reformation of the world. In Anglo-American thought it was accepted that "all men are created equal" in the sense that in the state of nature no one has the authority to dominate another, and that everyone has the right to labor and possess property because everyone has the right to self-preservation. Rousseau accepted the principle of equality, but he depicted the modern world of private property and unequal social classes as a deviation from the primitive conditions of noble savagery, and he doubted that ownership was an incentive to work and progress. As the French Revolution began to radicalize along Rousseauistic aims, the aristocracy lost its status and privileges and a general assault was waged on all forms of social distinctions. Adams's response, first in a series of newspaper articles, was published as the *Davila* book. Here he sought to explain why, in contrast to Rousseau's claim of natural equality, society will always produce different class strata because people are driven by a desire to outdo one another and achieve recognition. "We are told that our friends, the National Assembly of France," scoffs Adams, "have abolished all distinctions. But be not deceived, my dear countrymen. Impossibilities cannot be performed. Have they leveled all fortunes, and equally divided all property? Have they made all men and women equally elegant, wise, and beautiful? . . . . Have they blotted out all memories, the names, places of abode, and illustrious actions of their ancestors?"

Criticisms leveled at Adams, during his time and even today, charge him with being blind to the newness of America and continuing to think in terms of Old World social categories. Why disperse power among different class strata when America remained an undifferentiated mass of people? Why think of conflict when America enjoys a consensus of shared values?

The answer is that Adams believed America would replicate Europe's conflicting social structure and produce "monarchical," "aristocratical," and "democratical" constituencies that preferred to be governed by either a single leader, an educated elite, or the will of the majority. Adams could care less that America lacked a feudal heritage and established aristocracy, for he saw the universal "passion for distinction" as an irrepressible urge in any social order. Adams's critics charged that he was advocating aristocratic rule when he was describing why it would be not so much desirable as inevitable. Even patriotism, a fundamental virtue in classical thought, evolved from the emotions of pride, and thus the veterans of the American Revolution, who had organized the Cincinnati Society, will not retire into obscurity but instead must enjoy the limelight. Adams once distrusted the Cincinnati as a narrow interest faction, but he came to see its status-conscious behavior as evidence of his psychological theories:

> Perhaps it may be said, that in America we have no distinctions of ranks, and therefore shall not be liable to those divisions and discords which spring from them; but have we not labourers, yeoman, gentlemen, esquires . . . and are these distinctions established by law? Have they not been established by our ancestors from the first plantation of the country, and are not those distinctions as earlier desired and sought, as titles, garters, and ribbons are in any nation of Europe? . . . We may call this passion for distinction childish and silly; and its Author made it so, undoubtedly for wise purposes. . . . All we can say in America is that legal distinctions, titles, powers, and privileges are not hereditary; but that the disposition to artificial distinctions . . . is ardent in America, we may see by the institution of the Cincinnati. There is not a more remarkable phenomenon in universal history, nor in universal nature, than this order. The officers of the army, who had voluntarily engaged in a service under the authority of the people, whose creation and preservation was upon the principle that the body of the people were the only fountain of power and of honour; officers too as enlightened and as virtuous as ever served in any army; the moment they had answered the end of their creation, instituted titles and ribbons, and hereditary descents, by their own authority only, without the consent or knowledge of the people, or their representatives or legislatures.

Adams had no patience with the French Enlightenment and its conviction that *liberté, égalité, et fraternité* would replace authority,

hierarchy, and rivalry. Instead, he drew upon the Scottish Enlightenment of David Hume and Adam Smith. The Scots were less
interested in showing how political virtue is to be sustained than in
explaining how wealth is created and liberty preserved in an emer-
gent market economy. Adams turned to Smith's *A Theory of Moral
Sentiments* to appreciate how behavior is socially driven. But while
Smith departed from the older notion of political virtue, he did try
to sustain the imperatives of moral philosophy as he wrote on political economy. He hoped that somehow the temptations of materi-
alism would not completely rid the world of conscience and ethical
behavior. Unlike the atheist Hume, Smith retained a Christian sensibility and expected that the human capacity for "self-command"
would save society from the corruptions of commerce that had
been the nightmare of classical thought. But to Adams the self
could not command itself since it belonged to, and was shaped by,
society, and what would save society were properly constructed
political institutions. The lesson of Rome, he wrote, "may lead us to
doubt that commerce corrupts manners." Adams agreed with
Hume that economic development could bring progress and that
the older stoicism was too austere a philosophy, that, indeed, the
spartan state had smothered the lifeblood of liberty instead of nur-
turing it. Smith thought that the free market would produce the
wealth of nations that made justice possible because of a saving
moral sense lingering in the human faculties. But Adams was less
sanguine and more troubled, believing that modern democracy fed
the appetite for affluence. In the "late war," he noted in reference to
the Revolution, Americans delighted in the influx of huge amounts
of money, and "without the least degree of prudence, foresight, consideration, or measure, rushed headlong into a greater degree of
luxury than ought to have crept in in a hundred years." With amazing prescience, Adams predicted America becoming an acquisitive
society:

> A free people are the most addicted to luxury of any: that
> equality which they enjoy, and in which they glory, inspires
> them with sentiments which hurry them into luxury. A citizen

perceives his fellow-citizen, whom he holds his equal [to] have a better coat or hat, a better house or horse, than himself, and sees his neighbors are struck with it, talk of it, and respect him for it; he cannot bear it; he must and will be upon a level with him. Such an emulation as this takes place in every neighborhood, in every family; among artisans, husbandmen, labourers, as much as between dukes and marquisses, and more—these are all nearly equal in dress, and are now distinguished by other marks. Declamations, oratory, poetry, sermons against luxury, riches, and commerce, will never have much effect: the most rigorous sumptuary laws will have little more.

THE SPECTATORIAL TURN: ADAMS AND SHAKESPEARE

One cannot overestimate the originality of Adams's political philosophy. In orthodox classical theory it was assumed that monarchy would be guided by honor, aristocracy by moderation, despotism by fear, and democracy by virtue. Adams turns political philosophy on its head. When he tells us that the citizen perceives what his fellow citizens possess and judges himself according to how he is perceived in his own possessions, he anticipates by centuries what our modern thinkers call "triangular desire." It is the urge to have and possess not for reasons of need but for reasons of prestige, the wishing for some object only because one's rival wishes it, and hence the desired object creates two other desires in different subjects. It is curious that Adams became a critic of French philosophy because today it is precisely French thinkers like René Girard, Pierre Bourdieu, Guy du Bord, and Giles Deluze who are writing in the tradition that he first formulated. They too are writing about the ineluctability of power, the agency of desire, the craving for distinction, the presence of rivalry, envy, hierarchy, emulation, fashion, consumption, vanity, inquietude, and society as the spectacle of the fetishism of commodities and the theater of possessiveness, all of which affirms Adams's conviction that everything turns on the "attention of the public," the "eyes of the spectator," and the "language of signs." Such contemporary French thinkers have been categorized as "stratification theorists," a label that easily fits Adams, who centuries ago recognized that democracy, rather than overcoming inequality, reproduces it. No less than contemporary thinkers, Adams was a shrewd student of power, and he presages their awareness that when knowledge fails we are left with power and its effects. Hence he quotes Shakespeare: "Take but degree away, untune that string / And hark! What discord follows! Each thing meets / In mere oppugnancy . . . / Then everything includes itself in power." Adams was trying to make us aware in the eighteenth century what contemporary poststructuralists teach us today: the presence of democracy by no means resolves the presence of power. For telling the truth about reality, his opponents accused him of being a reactionary monarchist.

Adams's *Davila* contained numerous long passages from *Troilus and Cressida* and several other of Shakespeare's plays. In Shakespeare politics is cold and cunning, splendid in gesture and often petty in purpose, and society requires degrees, differences, and distinctions. Adams could readily appreciate that in most of Shakespeare's political plays there is no difference in the behavior of characters living in either a monarchy or a republic. But he could also appreciate in the playwright what he appreciated in the economist Adam Smith: the possibility that in modern politics the visual would replace any vestige of the intellectual, that what you see is what you get.

Centuries earlier Machiavelli also insisted that "men as a whole judge more with their eyes" because "to see belongs to everyone," and the Italian philosopher counted upon the reputation of virtuous leaders to influence the community. Adams, however, believed that "the springs of conduct and opinion are not always so clear and pure," and motives cannot be seen and may remain unknown. Adams made us aware of what modes, if not motives, of behavior would enjoy reputation, and in doing so he anticipated modern thinkers like Thorstein Veblen and Pierre Bourdieu in foreseeing that wealth, glamour, and leisure would be emulated and enjoy recognition. Adams drew upon Smith's *A Theory of Moral Sentiments*, which focused on the spectatorial dimension of human relations to suggest that benevolence could emerge from a sense of sympathy people have toward others as their imaginations enable them to empathize with those they see suffering. Adams was less interested in altruism than in the prospect that we ourselves depend upon how others see us; our self is formed in the process of imaging what others would be thinking of us if we were in their place. To the extent that the "other" beyond ourselves becomes the judge, politics will be determined by public opinion that is itself shaped by visual images.

In older Christian thought, matters of the spirit could not be seen, and thus one must trust "the Word." Even in Adams's era, among many thinkers of the Enlightenment, seeing and gazing were regarded as befitting art and the theater, but modern politics would be a matter of pen and tongue, media of communication that required the reflections of the mind. With Adams, however, we are in the world that Shakespeare put on the stage and that our contemporary theorists call "the society of the spectacle," an environment of seeing and being looked upon. "Why," he asked, "are the personal accomplishments of beauty, elegance, and grace, held in such esteem by mankind? Is it merely from the pleasure which is received from the sight of these attributes? By no means. The taste for such delicacies is not universal; in those who feel the most lively sense of them, it is but a slight sensation, and of the shortest continuance; but those attractions command the notice and attention of the public; they draw the eyes of the spectators."

Adams's prescience is amazing. In the presidential elections of 1960, John F. Kennedy and Richard Nixon had a series of debates. Many of those who heard the debates on the radio judged Nixon the winner, but when they viewed a rerun on television, they changed their minds and concluded that Kennedy had won. Henceforth the American public would "watch" presidential debates, the eye would be judge and jury, and seeing was believing. The spectatorial dimension in human relations may be universal. Today in contemporary China, capitalism has sprung forth from communism, and the wealthy elites not only enjoy power but feel the need to display their riches before a camera. "To get rich," exhorted Deng Xiaoping, "is glorious." Karl Marx, where art thou now?

Today among the American public John Adams is popular as an endearing human being and admirable president. Among some academic intellectuals, however, he commands more respect in France than in America. The leading authority on American colonial history, Gordon S. Wood, regards Adams as "irrevelant" since his "anomalous" projections of distinct social orders never materialized in American history. Sean Wilentz, once a radical historian who saw class conflict everywhere in American history, now chides Adams for believing in such a specter.

But as Arthur O. Lovejoy pointed out years ago, Adams anticipates Thorstein Veblen's take on modern society, and a Veblenian could point out to Adams's critics that although America had no inherited aristocracy, it did have a leisure class whose wealth enjoyed power and exercised influence in government and throughout society. And one might remind the Marxist that the absence of class conflict does not mean the absence of class domination as the lower levels of society "emulate" those above. Social historians are ill at ease with Adams, for they are convinced that history happens "from the bottom up," while he tried to demonstrate that power and deference operate from the top down. The ultimate test of the validity of Adams's ideas takes us to the subject of the French Revolution.

"TURNING US INTO BEASTS": ADAMS VERSUS ROUSSEAU AND JEFFERSON

When Adams first heard of the outbreak of the revolution in France, in the summer of 1789, he speculated what might happen "in a nation of thirty million atheists." Long before the event he had a running quarrel with Rousseau, who insisted that the norm of the "state of nature" should serve to criticize all existing institutions and that the new era of popular democracy will find its expression in the "general will." Adams read closely Rousseau's *Discourse sur l'inegalité* and made witty notes in the margins of the text. How can the general will be the "voice of God" if the majority is fifty-one and the minority forty-nine? Does God change His mind from day to day? In Rousseau's general will, of course, there is no minority and no dissent; one must go along with it or be "forced to be free."

The eminent British historian Lord Acton once observed of Rousseau that he "had produced more effect with his pen than Aristotle, or Cicero, or Saint Augustine, or Saint Thomas Aquinas, or any other man who ever lived." Perhaps an exaggeration, but Madame de Staël may be closer to the truth when she noted: "Rousseau said nothing new, but set everything on fire."

Adams wrote his political treatises in hopes of preventing the fire from spreading to America. Rousseau's ringing claim that "man is born free, yet everywhere he is in chains," could hardly persuade a mind haunted by sin (or a modern Freudian wracked with the thought of unconscious desires). Rousseau first uttered the idea that would be repeated in the French criticisms of the American Constitution: Since people love liberty so much and would never abuse it, there need be no institutional controls and, like innocent animals, they should be free to roam at will. Exasperated, Adams writes to Rousseau, "Never before has so much wit been employed to turn us into beasts." Rousseau's extolling the innocence of the noble savage led Adams to respond: "Reading your work, one has the desire to walk on all fours."

Adams's sardonic commentary on Rousseau and his criticisms of the French Revolution made it appear that he was shedding tears for monarchy and aristocracy and wanted to see such institutions restored. Yet far from a backward-looking monarchist, Adams was a forward-looking institutionalist concerned with making government a more rational construction than the passion-swept people who compose it. Skeptical of the classical principle of noble self-renunciation, and of the Enlightenment's trust in reason, he believed that a well-devised government would be more reliable in dealing with power and conflict than all the "pious exhortations" about citizenship and virtue sprinkled in the texts of political philosophy. Nevertheless, Adams had to face the apparent contradiction that one of the country's most ardent champions of the American Revolution became one of the country's severest critics of the French Revolution. Adams's stance irritated French thinkers who had earlier seen, or thought they had seen, the ideals of their own Enlightenment triumphing in the American Revolution, a victory of "wisdom" over "prejudice, dogma, and superstition." Why did Adams refuse to see 1789 as a continuation of the "spirit of '76"?

One answer is that the French were attempting to realize what America had only been attempting to protect. His old friend Condorcet made the point when he grew impatient with Adams for refusing to understand that his people had to create what America had inherited. France, in contrast to America, had to declare their rights before they possessed them, and hence the older political structures had to make way for new possibilities in the regeneration of political society. How, then, to redeem society? On this question Adams's stance is unique in the history of political philosophy, and it can be appreciated by considering some other perspectives.

To redeem humankind from its endless civil wars, Niccolò Machiavelli looked to the prince to lead the way in establishing stability and making liberty possible. To overcome the perils of the state of nature, John Locke looked to America, where he saw "no such thing as money was anywhere known," and hence at society's beginning property represented honest labor. Facing the coming of industrial society, Karl Marx looked downward to the proletariat to redeem the world from misery and oppression. Reacting to the ravages of the French Revolution, Edmund Burke looked upward to the aristocracy to restore order and stability. Struck by Napoleon's march into Prussia, G. W. F. Hegel looked even further upward to the divine realm of "Spirit" unfolding in the destiny of the state to bring about the end of all conflict and dialectical contradiction. Where, then, did Adams look? He looked neither to a figure, a class, nor a philosophical idea. Instead, he offered the system and structure of government itself, one that went beyond the English Whig tradition by emphasizing the importance of the executive office, a nonredemptive system deliberately designed to prevent the monopolization of power, to restrain evil rather than to realize good.

Yet what Adams had to offer was as much part of the problem as its solution. With Adams's perspective, America has no message to a world that is struggling to become free before it has enjoyed the taste of freedom. Adams wanted the French to think about the constitution before they had won the revolution. The Jacobin Maximilien Robespierre, for whom the expression *terrorism* came into existence, put it better in taunting America: You want to end our revolution before we have truly had it. Are we dealing here with American hubris or French blindness?

Perhaps both. When Adams discussed the inevitability of an aristocratic stratum represented in a balanced government, he seemed to be indifferent to the utterly selfish and stubborn behavior of the nobles and how entrenched they remained in the corridors of French political power. Hence French thinkers sought the centralization of the power of the state as a means of purging the aristocracy. The right solution? Perhaps. Yet the means used to achieve revolutionary objectives often become the ends themselves. Centralized power may have done some good in curbing aristocracy, but it also made possible Robespierre and Napoleon. What was going on in France was truly a social revolution that divided class against class; yet in America all classes fought on the same side against the English, and on this side of the Atlantic it was not necessary to centralize power in a country that had abolished primogeniture, the right of property going to the oldest son, the institution upon which aristocracy perpetuated itself. Adams confronted a problem that has perplexed American history ever since. Having had no genuine class revolution, how could America comprehend the trials and turmoils of another country that had to experience one?

Yet remarkably, Adams turned out to be more Montesquieuian than the French thinkers themselves, who would denounce their own Charles-Louis de Montesquieu together with John Adams. As the revolution continued its bloody course, it proceeded to follow the very path that Adams had foreseen as suicidal in his *Defence*. Scornful of Montesquieu and Adams, the French Directory debated and dismissed their ideas as guillotines went up and heads fell down to the lusty roar of crowds. Rejecting Adams's *Defence* and Montesquieu's *The Spirit of Laws*, French revolutionaries proceeded to establish a direct national assembly without any mechanisms for the separation of powers. Heady with the dreams of Rousseau's "general will," the Paris Commune of 1793 went to bed with Reason and woke up with Robespierre.

Where, then, did the French go wrong? It is the conventional wisdom in history books that the French Declaration of the Rights of Man was "abstract" and our own Declaration of Independence "concrete." Such was far from Adams's critique, which was addressed more to the abstract notion of sovereignty.

Although the French saw themselves as breaking radically from the past, in one instance they were carrying it forward like an unfelt curse, and this is the concept of sovereignty. Originally an idea associated with monarchy and even despotism, French revolutionary thinkers assumed they could democratize the idea. Rousseau located sovereignty in the people themselves, and Abbe Sieyès in the nation, which he saw as a mystical force with a will of its own. "A nation cannot decide to be or not to be," he announced, in language that would have confounded Adams and the American framers, who were trying to bring a nation-state into being out of a collection of different colonies. In the American system of government there would be no clear source of sovereignty, no indisputable, incontestable, irresistible center of power. Adams reminded the French that there is no such thing as "the people" as an entity, for the masses of citizens do not come together, reason with similar thoughts, and reach common conclusions. The French sought to centralize sovereignty; the Americans settled for dividing it.

But Thomas Jefferson thought the people were sovereign and wise and the state subversive and wicked. And what was true of America would be true of France.

During the French Revolution, Adams's enemies found their voice in the *National Gazette*, where they hailed the Jacobins as Jeffersonianism in the streets. While Vice President Adams tried to convince the public that the French Revolution bore no resemblance to the American, Secretary of State Jefferson thought that the future of human freedom depended on the outcome of the French Revolution, even going so far as justifying the execution of the king as an "absolute necessity." Yet years earlier, when Jefferson and Adams were together serving diplomatic missions in Paris, they both doubted a successful revolution could take place in France, not only because of the inherited vices of the ancien régime but also because of the relaxed *moeurs* of the female sex.

The easy morality of French women posed a problem for Adams and Jefferson and other Americans in Paris, though not for the swinging Ben Franklin or the libertine Gouverneur Morris, who shared a mistress with Talleyrand. Prostitutes in the streets, courtesans in the salons, trysts in the carriages—what was a Puritan to do! Actually Adams was less offended than Jefferson by Parisian ladies, and he would write to Abigail of their cultural accomplishments while his Virginia counterpart complained of their decadence. But if a revolution required the virtue of "republican motherhood," France was in trouble. Adams's daughter was told by a French lady that mothers sent their young girls to a convent to remove them from the influence of *mauvaise femmes*. But it was not only women. The daughter remembers how her father, finding himself seated next to an eighty-year-old ambassador married to a fifteen-year-old, "was very much disgusted at the match."

During the early years of the revolution, Jefferson forgot his reservations about Parisian *moeurs* and was more delighted than disgusted with events in France. He had no qualms about those who were sent to the guillotine as "enemies" of the "committee of public safety." On the contrary, "the liberty of the whole earth was depending on the issue of the contest, and was there ever such a prize won with so little innocent blood," he wrote to a friend in 1793, convinced that the insurgents in Paris were simply carrying out the spirit of the American Revolution. "My own affections have been deeply wounded by some of the martyrs to the cause," he wrote in reference to the Terror, "but rather than it should have failed, I would have seen half the earth desolated. Were there but an Adam and Eve left in every country, and left free, it would be better than it now is." Jefferson, the apostle of liberty and tolerance in America, became the defender of tyranny and terrorism in France.

Years later Jefferson reconsidered his mistaken attitudes, admitting that the American Revolution may have been different after all. As to Adams, he was not one to gloat over his prescience, even though his *Defence* predicted what happens when power without opposition carries out its inexorable tendency to grow, consolidate, exclude, and dominate. The French Jacobins assumed there would be no problem with power and tyranny once aristocracy had been abolished, just as communist revolutionaries in the twentieth century assumed there would be no problem with exploitation and oppression once property was abolished. The French Revolution needed fewer barricades and more balance, the Bolshevik Revolution fewer Soviets and more conflicts.

The French Revolution was the first major event that challenged America to face the world and comprehend what was going on in the throes of a violent upheaval against the old order. Significantly, it was Adams's Virginian antagonists who failed to grasp the meaning of events. Many of the pro-French anti-Federalists, who were staunchly antistatist in America, ardently supported a revolution that did more to centralize power than to create the conditions for liberty and freedom. Did the American Francophiles think that the French Revolution would return power to the people in the provinces? Even before 1789, Adams and Hamilton tried to teach America that the cult of the democratic people may easily lead to the cult of the despotic state, a warning made in the first *Federalist* and throughout the *Defence*. The English historian Herbert Butterfield has best expressed the phenomenon:

> Whether the French Revolution led the world to democracy is a question that has still to be decided. There can be no doubt of one of its effects: it led to the development of a more powerful type of state. It produced a state more calculated for efficiency, more highly organized, more wide in its competence, more terrifying in its power than any which then existed; and it made government more irresistible from the fact that henceforth government was to claim to be the incontrovertible agent of the new god, the organic people.

On the French Revolution Adams's major antagonist was Thomas Paine, the popular author and libertarian hero to later generations of

Americans, including President Ronald Reagan. In a letter to Washington, written from Paris in July 1796, Paine claimed that he had heard from John Jay that Adams made the remark: "As Mr. Washington had no child, the presidency should be made hereditary in the family." There is no evidence that Adams ever uttered such sentiment. On the contrary, what he did write in the *Defence* led to the exact opposite conclusion. If a republican regime, he warned, does not adopt the right constitution, "it will be the misfortune of those individuals and families as much as the public; for what consolation can it be to a man, to think that his whole life, and that of his son and grandson, must be spent in unceasing misery and warfare, for the sake only of a possibility that his great-grandson may become a despot!"

It was not the legacy of monarchism but the lessons of liberalism that Adams tried to teach the world. He sought to demonstrate that conflicts can be controlled by a balanced, "mixed" constitution. But it would be misleading to suggest that revolutionary France—or for that matter twentieth-century Russia, China, and Cuba—needed the wisdom of John Adams and the truths of American liberalism. Adams's legacy, as profound as it is, leaves America with only half a message. The Constitution that he defended may teach the world how to consolidate a revolution; it has yet to teach the world how to create one.

4

The Halo of Washington, the Shadow of Jefferson

"ANTI-FEDERALISM, JACOBINISM, REBELLION"

In the history of the American presidency, the office of the vice president has enjoyed little attention and experienced less controversy. The case of John Adams is the exception. Since the growing opposition to the Federalists dared not attack President Washington, it took after Adams with a vengeance. Adams's two texts, the *Defence* and the *Discourses on Davila*, led to the suspicion that to be antirevolutionary is to be anti-American. A person hostile to the French Revolution must be incapable of accepting the American Revolution and be secretly plotting its overthrow. The opposition journal *Aratus* subjected Adams to a loyalty oath: "Whoever owns the principles of one revolution must cherish those of others ; and the person who draws a distinction between them is either blinded by prejudice, or boldly denies what at the bar of reason, cannot be refuted."

That Adams failed to support the French Revolution also sowed the suspicion that he would urge President Washington to take the country into war against France, a suspicion that remained when he became president. In the early 1790s, while France and England were at war and both belligerents seized American vessels, the vice president agreed with Washington that America must practice a policy of strict neutrality. The proclamation of neutrality meant the abrogation of the mutual alliance treaty with France in 1778, when America sought French support in its struggle against England. But in the 1790s revolutionary France no longer represented the old regime with which America had signed the treaty, and the young Republic had no intention of getting dragged into a war between two European powers. Yet France now needed the covert support of America just as America once needed the support of France, and the Girondins, a moderate revolutionary party in Paris, sent across the Atlantic Edmond-Charles Genet to seek such support by any means possible, even if it meant circumventing the Washington administration that officially represented the American people.

Young, dashing, charming, Citizen Genet arrived in the United States in April 1793, welcomed by the enthusiastic American Francophiles. Genet was sent with instructions to arouse the people of Louisiana and Canada behind the French Revolution, to win support in Kentucky, a key state to the control of the Mississippi River, and to encourage privateering against British merchant vessels. Adams had known the Genet family in France and he watched the son's activities in America with apprehension. He ultimately saw Genet as a sleek, shallow person with no judgment, "little accustomed to reflect upon his own or his fellow creatures' heart." Genet went too far when he decided to address Congress directly over the heads of the president, vice president, and secretary of state. Having alienated the administration, which was moving to have him recalled, Genet continued to travel through the country to the applause of street crowds. Even Republicans realized he was jeopardizing their cause. His mission a failure, Genet had the good sense to stay away from France where, after the fall of the Girondins and the rise of the Jacobins, he might have faced the guillotine. He fell in love and married Governor George Clinton's daughter and settled in upstate New York, where he lived happily ever after.

After the Genet controversy subsided, America's attention shifted from France to England. During Washington's administration, the country's trade increased dramatically, to almost 100,000 tons annually. But America's merchant vessels faced assault and capture by the English navy in the Caribbean and on the high seas. The provocations incensed the public, and Washington sent John Jay to London to negotiate a treaty. Many Americans had no patience for negotiation and demanded a declaration of war. When word spread that the Jay Treaty won few concessions for America (demands for the right of neutral trade, protection of seamen, resolution of Indian hostilities in the northwest territories), abuse was heaped upon Jay. In Philadelphia he dangled from a post in effigy, and "hung from the neck by a hemp string was a copy of *Defence of the Constitutions.*" The Jay Treaty would haunt Adams into his presidency.

Adams's eight years as vice president in Philadelphia, the temporary capital of the United States, were solitary and lonely. A voluble mind accustomed to holding forth on any subject, he had to sit in silence while the Senate debated. In no position to give public speeches or to submit statements to the press, he consoled himself by reading Tacitus and Homer and the Philadelphia newspapers. Abigail for budgetary reasons remained in Braintree. The salary of $5,000 was far short of affording the Adams family a comfortable house in Philadelphia.

Abigail and John looked forward to their weekly exchange of letters. She chided him for his scoffing at Mary Wollstonecraft and the feminist aspirations to equality. "Confess the truth," she wrote, and admit that when you are "sick of the ambition, the intrigues, and duplicity" of politics, you can "retire to the simplicity, the gentleness and tenderness of the female character." Abigail had good reason to say as much when hearing her husband complain that maybe Jefferson should be vice president where he could do neither good nor harm. But out of office, having resigned as secretary of state, "his mind is now poisoned with passion, prejudice, and faction."

A faction was synonymous with a political party, and neither was a respectable idea at this time. Meanwhile, Jefferson and the Virginians induced Philip Freneau's *National Gazette* to go after Hamilton as well as Adams, and Hamilton retaliated in John Fenno's *Gazette of the United States*. As vice president, Adams did not involve himself in the newspaper war, while Jefferson worked behind the scenes as though he were above the fray.

In the election of 1792, the Virginian opposition to the Federalists Washington, Adams, and Hamilton worked with elements in

New York and Pennsylvania to have their candidates elected to Congress. There was even an attempt to support Governor Clinton as the next vice president and thereby dispose of Adams. While Hamilton and Jefferson went at each other in their respective newspapers, Washington said not a word and received the vote of every elector, and Adams, also maintaining dignity, managed to stave off Clinton's bid for the vice presidency by a vote of seventy-seven to fifty.

It was unclear who would succeed Washington in 1796. Jefferson began to call his opposition "the Republican interests," still reluctant to use the term *party*. The Republicans hated Hamilton for his financial policies and Adams for his critical views on the French Revolution and on democracy in general. The Federalists felt that the democratic impulse would, if not controlled, assault property, as it did at the local level during the period of the Articles of Confederation. The Virginia opposition trusted the local and feared the national, convinced that the people could do no wrong and government could do no right. In the early 1790s, small associations developed in some states that were vaguely political but more often fraternal or philanthropic and decidedly not aligned with either the Federalists or the Republicans. But the Democratic Society of Philadelphia emerged to voice the case for the French Revolution whose enemies in America were suspected of betraying the principles of republican government. Ironically, by 1794 the French Revolution had betrayed itself with its terror and the reign of pure virtue that prohibited all liberty and license. In the summer of that year, an insurgency took place in Pennsylvania in the name of liberty and liquor.

The Whiskey Rebellion shook the Washington administration and tested the authority of the national government. In western Pennsylvania, whiskey was the major commodity, and when the federal government imposed an excise tax on it, "Democratic Societies" protested a levy that fell so heavily on one part of the country. Their remonstrances having failed, the rebels threatened to arm themselves and march on Philadelphia. The president called upon the states to raise twelve thousand soldiers. The response was overwhelming as Washington headed the volunteers with Hamilton second in command. During the late summer, the country waited nervously for reports of bloody battles. But the insurgents backed down, and Hamilton pursued a dozen remaining recalcitrants into the woods. Adams was relieved and overjoyed. "An army of 15,000 militia, so easily raised from four states only, to go upon such an enterprise," he noted, "ought to be a terrible phenomenon to Anti-Federal citizens as well. . . . Anti-Federalism, Jacobinism and rebellion are drooping their heads very much discouraged." But Adams proved to be prescient in telling Abigail that such uprisings "may become fashionable again" in a country still without a clear political identity. Indeed they would, in the same part of the country, in an uprising several years later that would lose Pennsylvania to the Republicans and Adams's bid for reelection as president.

"THE OLD MAN WILL MAKE A GOOD PRESIDENT"

In Adams's era, the American people knew they were living under a republic, and some expected that before long the country would become a mass democracy with the franchise available even to propertyless white males. But from 1789 to 1796, America was also living under the first and only example of charismatic authority in American history. Washington's election and reelection to the office of the presidency with the complete unanimity of the country reflected the phenomenon of charisma, the magnetic appeal of a leader who inspires awe and stands above politics and its accusations. Washington could have easily served a third term and possibly more, but his willingness to leave office at the height of his popularity was the greatest political gift a leader could give a people. In future American politics, presidents would cling to office when caught in a political or sexual scandal and be willing to face impeachment rather than relinquish power. The behavior of Washington is all the more amazing since Adams and the framers of the Constitution were reluctant to rely upon virtuous character in the new republic.

Yet the effect on the country of Washington's retirement in 1796 may have proven the framers correct. Knowing Washington would no longer be around left people free to vent their passions and prejudices, and American politics has its origins in the very emotions that Adams had examined in his *Discourses*: jealousy, suspicion, rivalry, resentment, and accusation. Such negative politics may have reflected the healthy clashes of a democratic society. But politics involves organization, and where there is organization there is oligarchy. The move against John Adams as the possible next president was made in the name of the people, but it was led by a cabal that listened to one person only. With Adams and the Federalists on the defensive regarding the French Revolution, the Jay Treaty, and the Whiskey Rebellion, the Republicans developed the politics of aspersion, and the Federalists were not above responding in kind.

Four eminent figures stood out as possible successors to Washington: Adams, Hamilton, Jay, and Jefferson. Hamilton commanded respect, but his cold style of aloof politics won little popularity. Jay's chances had been undermined by the controversial diplomatic treaty with England. The decision America faced was between Adams and Jefferson, neither of whom actively campaigned for the office. But their supporters did, and the election of 1796 proved to be as scurrilous as it was vicious. Jeffersonians raised the familiar charge of monarchism on the part of a vice president whose alleged love for nobility led him to be called "His Rotundity." Federalists attacked Jefferson's alleged atheism and his friendly views toward revolutionary France.

France had again become a factor in American politics. With the Jay Treaty seeming so pro-British, the French Directory debated whether to declare war upon America. Instead it decided to send over an official, authorized to intervene in the American elections on the side of the Republicans. In Pennsylvania and elsewhere some citizens began to sport the tricolor cockade hat of the Parisian revolutionaries, and rumors were rife of a French fleet on its way to New York. Literacy was higher in northern colonial America than it is today in America, and many Americans read in the newspapers about what was happening in France: the terror, regicide, guillotines, and fear of a peasant uprising. Are the French headed for our shores?

If the French were not coming, Hamilton feared the Republicans were. Hamilton had once respected Adams and intended to support him in the election. But with the French scare, he feared Jefferson all the more. Hamilton worried that New England voters would waste their second ballot by scattering it after they gave their first to Adams. At the time members of the electoral college chosen by the states cast not one vote for a two-candidate ticket but two votes for two different candidates, one of whom had to be from another state. Hamilton urged them to vote solidly for Thomas Pinckney, a former general from South Carolinia, as well as for Adams to assure Jefferson's defeat. With the votes going equally to the two Federalists, there was the chance that Pinckney might defeat the favorite Adams, which Hamilton preferred to a Jefferson victory. Hamilton's advice was disregarded, but it did result in diminishing Adams's vote, who came out ahead of Jefferson by only three electoral ballots, seventy-two to sixty nine, with Pinckney receiving fifty-nine.

Hamilton was seen as acting more out of jealousy toward Adams than worry about Jefferson. Abigail and the new president would never forgive the former Treasury secretary for his meddling with the New England vote. Indeed, the hostility of Adams toward Hamilton is peculiar in that both stood for many of the same ideas, including a strong national government and a suspicion of democracy and its susceptibility to demagogy. Yet even though both had deeper differences with Jefferson, Adams and Hamilton became bitter enemies. Adams saw Hamilton as too trusting of the "rich, well-born, and able" and too enamored with banks and monetary policy. Hamilton also seemed to have an itch for military adventurism, urging America into a war with France and seeking an army command so he could march on western American territories claimed by France and Spain. The circumstance of Hamilton's illegitimate birth brought forth a cruel utterance of Adams toward "the bastard brat of a Scottish peddler." For his part, Hamilton never seemed to accept Adams as president and published a harsh pamphlet describing him as "incapable of leading a party or governing a nation." Both sought to lead the Federalists, and while Adams was regarded as "heir apparent" as vice president, Hamilton, the former brilliant military officer, could not help but see himself as Washington's true successor.

Ironically, what Adams had admonished in his political philosophy were precisely the emotions now on display in the political arena: ambition, envy, desire, glory, the passion for distinction. At that time, it was regarded as unseemly even to let it be known that one wanted to be president. Rather than scrambling for it, the office should seek the person. In theory, especially ancient classical theory, politics and political involvement would bring out the best in people as they dedicated their efforts to civic responsibility and the public good. But in America, in Adams's era, politics had the opposite effect. With emerging political factions having no loyal traditions, friends and neighbors turned against one another. "Nothing affects me so much as to see friends set up in opposition to me," Adams lamented, convinced that with the election of 1796 "all Confidence between Man and Man is Suspended for a Time."

As president of the Senate, Adams found himself in the awkward position of announcing himself the president-elect. He also had to inform Abigail, snowbound in Quincy in the dead of winter, that he had won the election. The Adams family was overcome with worry and joy, wondering about the difficult times ahead and at the same time delighted by the triumph of their husband and father. Adams was happy to report that even before the outcome of the election an anti-Federalist senator had remarked: "The old man will make a good President, too. . . . But we shall have to check him a little now and then. That will be all." He also knew that on Inauguration Day the hero of the hour would still be the outgoing president George Washington. "He seemed to me," wrote Adams the day after, "to enjoy the triumph over me. Methought I heard him say, 'Ay! I am fairly out and you are fairly in. See which of us will be the happiest!'"

THE INAUGURAL AND THE CABINET

On the day he was to be sworn into office, Adams did not make the mistake he made as the vice president by strutting into the Senate in pomp and ceremony. He wore a simple gray suit; no jewels, no buckles, no sash, no sword. He called off a procession that was to head his carriage, and he ordered returned to the stable the four white horses of the outgoing president. Adams stepped up to the podium as the symbol of republicanism in all its simplicity and moderation.

The inaugural address appealed to the nation's pride. It began with the subject dearest to his heart, the country's struggle for independence from England, reminding the audience how common people "broke to pieces the chains" that had once bound them into submission. He made clear his distance from Old World institutions with their "robes and diamonds," and he even praised the people for their virtue and their capacity for knowledge and enlightenment, thereby forgetting the doubts he had expressed about such thoughts in his own writings. It was the "good sense, presence of mind, resolution, [and] integrity" of the people that made possible the adoption of the Constitution. Washington came in for splendid praise for steering the country through its uncertain beginnings and winning the respect of the world. As would other inaugural addresses throughout history, Adams's called for reconciliation, appealing to different classes, sections, factions, and denominations to come together and put aside the spirit of dissidence. In foreign affairs, he was determined to maintain peace, and to the consternation of the Federalist Anglophiles and the delight of the Republican Gallicans, he expressed a "personal esteem for the French nation" based on his years of living there and his desire to maintain friendly relations. The speech ended, as almost all inaugurals would, with gratitude toward God for the blessings bestowed on America.

The speech received a thunder of applause from Congress, and as Adams was leaving the hall Washington headed toward him to wish "a happy, successful, and honorable" administration. The self-scrutinizing Adams wondered whether he tried to take too much credit for the Constitution or appeared to speak too much about himself. When militant Federalists complained that he was too conciliatory toward the Republicans, Adams mused to Abigail that he could resign and turn over the office to Jefferson.

If the halo of Washington hung over Adams's career as vice president, the shadow of Jefferson hung over his four years as president.

Adams was a mere three-vote president, and as second in the electoral count, Jefferson became vice president. Jefferson visited Adams to congratulate him, but there is no record of the conversation. The new vice president wrote a letter to his old antagonist that implied the possibility of a rapprochement, but it fell into the dustbin of history without Adams ever seeing it.

Jefferson regarded Adams as a barrier to Hamilton's ambitions, and in the letter he warned the president that due to the closeness of the election he should expect "a trick worthy of the subtlety of your arch-friend in New York" who will most likely work to discredit the administration. He showed the letter to Madison, who advised against sending it on the grounds that it could backfire. When and if the Republicans organize against the administration, Madison pointed out, the president could go public with the letter and show how they had betrayed the "confidence and friendship" they once promised. Two years later, in 1798, in the thick of the Adams administration, Madison felt confirmed in his doubts about the president, regarding him as "rash," a "hot-head," a "perfect Quixotte as a Statesman." Compared to the prudent Washington, Adams appeared too passionate, behaving with the very "zeal" that the *Federalist* authors had condemned in politics.

Adams entered the presidency with a double burden. Hamilton could hardly bare to think of Adams running successfully for a second term, and the Republicans could hardly bare to think of either Adams or Hamilton succeeding to become the next president. The most eminent name among the Federalists, Alexander Hamilton, was not in the president's corner.

Nor, it turned out, were members of his cabinet. In American history a new president generally cleans house, and former cabinet members are long gone before he arrives. But Adams had no precedent to follow and decided to keep the cabinet pretty much intact. Those who went to work for Washington were rather mediocre since the rancor of politics kept most talented people away from Philadelphia. One old-time historian, who happened to be a Jeffersonian, wrote of the predicament: "Ali Baba among his Forty Thieves is no more deserving of sympathy than John Adams shut up within the seclusion of his Cabinet." Adams didn't have forty cabinet members; three major ones were enough.

Timothy Pickering was kept on as secretary of state, a position Washington offered to him after it had been turned down by six others. Pickering was a bureaucratic functionary, a stickler for details with little patience for the subtleties of diplomacy. Under Washington as an emissary to the Seneca tribe, he did a competent and fair job of concluding a treaty with Native Americans. But Pickering could be consumed by his anti-Republican zeal, and he rarely got along with subordinates. Denouncing Adams's policy of moderation self-righteously, the secretary of state felt himself more right than the president whom he served.

Oliver Wolcott, Adams's secretary of Treasury, was more amiable but less honest and direct than Pickering, so cautious and discreet that he preferred to be told what to do than to know what to do. Like Pickering, Wolcott lived under financial pressure and had to depend upon his government job. Complacent, Wolcott would never think of rocking the boat, a yes-man who would rather please than provoke. Significantly, Adams's cabinet lacked what his own mind enjoyed: self-interrogation and creative tension.

Secretary of War James McHenry was an easygoing Irishman, all charm and cheer. Educated in Ireland, a writer of poetry, McHenry became a surgeon and served bravely during the Revolution. Around the Washington circle of sobriety, McHenry could be counted upon to break the ice and be the life of the party. Whether he served well the office of secretary of war is still debated by historians. When a war crisis arose in 1798, some Federalists claimed he was not up to the job. Two years later Adams dismissed McHenry, though not necessarily on grounds of incompetence.

The three major cabinet members became a drag on the Adams administration. Appointed by Washington, they actually became the creatures of Hamilton, who did much to promote their careers and to whom they listened more than to their own president. On some issues they publicly disagreed with Adams, but instead of resigning they stayed in office and worked against official policy. To this day, historians are unsure whether Adams was aware that his cabinet of supposedly dedicated public servants was less than loyal. His decision to keep them probably had to do with his desire to establish continuity with the previous Washington administration and to begin to build a corps of civil-service professionals whose appointment would not turn on the whims of politics. But Adams, unlike Washington, listened to his secretaries only to consider differing points of view, for he had little confidence in their abilities in dealing with delicate domestic issues. In keeping with custom, he did solicit their written opinions, but he learned early on that cabinet advice would be partisan and more personal than reflective. Adams preferred to make his own decisions, kept them to himself, and announced them when the timing was ripe. Such tactics may have cost him politically. Members of both parties resented not being informed, and Adams seemed naive in the last months of his administration when he shuttled back and forth to Quincy, presumably assuming that his cabinet would carry on his policies. But Adams, steeped in the writings of Tacitus, Machiavelli, and Bolingbroke, prized the imperative of leadership. "The unity, consistency, promptitude, secrecy, and activity of the whole executive authority," he wrote privately in 1797, "are so essential to my system of republican government, that without them there can be no peace, order, liberty, or property in society." Adams was trying to balance the leadership he had valued in enlightened monarchies with the freedom he valued even more in modern republics. He saw no hypocrisy in believing in the importance of dynamic leadership even in a coming democracy. Subjects without leaders may deliberate, but they cannot take decisive action, or, just as important, have the good sense to wait and delay—which would be characteristic of Adams's foreign policy.

A "PINCHED" PRESIDENT

In March 1797, Adams moved into the president's house in Philadelphia that had previously been occupied by Washington. He was distressed, he wrote Abigail, to find that the furniture "belonging to the public is in the most deplorable conditions." The president not only had to pay rent for a house left in shambles but also to pay for the horses and carriages. Congress allotted $14,000 for new furniture, but Adams's salary was only $25,000 annually. The president felt "pinched" as he warned his wife of necessary expenses and purchases. "There is not a chair fit to sit in," he wrote, and "the beds and bedding are in a woeful pickle." So were the servants, who used the vacant house as the scene "of the most scandalous drunkenness and disorder . . . that was ever heard of."

The house was vacant in other ways. Abigail must come at once. "I've never wanted your advice and assistance more in my life," he wrote to her in Quincy. Abigail stayed to be with Adams's aged, dying mother, and left the following month for Philadelphia. Abigail found life in the president's house arduous and demanding, having to spend several hours a day keeping company with visitors, dutifully listening while suppressing a yawn. No wonder, she reflected, that George Washington looked forward to retirement.

In his early days in office, Adams found himself deluged with applications for jobs. Washington had also had to deal with bundles of letters, mostly from revolutionary veterans. Those reaching Adams came from all sorts of Americans: destitute families, a parent in need of money for a child's education, an aged couple with no savings, relatives, friends, and friends of friends. One letter delighted Adams no end. It was actually written by his son John Quincy to his mother. The son assured her that he would never think of soliciting an office in government simply because his father had become president. To be tempted to such a wish would be "totally destitute of a personal sense of delicacy." Delighted with the letter, Abigail sent it on to John, who showed it to others and stated it "is the most most beautiful thing I ever read." Shortly afterward Abigail was also delighted that young John had fallen in love, and she urged him to be married before leaving for Portugal, where his father had appointed him ambassador.

John Quincy Adams would go on to become America's sixth president, but like his father his career was more remarkable before and after he served in the executive office. Young Adams turned out to be America's greatest secretary of state, the author of important addresses still read by students of diplomacy and also the actual author of the Monroe Doctrine, which would inform European powers that the Western Hemisphere lay in America's sphere of influence. After his presidency, Quincy Adams led the struggle against slavery while serving in Congress, and as a lawyer he defended Afro-Americans in the *Amistad* affair involving an uprising on a slave ship.

The historian Henry Adams proudly claims that antislavery sentiment ran through the family like an inherited gene. John Adams belonged to the American Abolition Society, but neither father nor son could address the issue of racism directly while president. Abigail, however, could do so, and she relished writing a letter to John when she was back in Quincy.

Abigail had directed a small black youth, a household servant named James, to a local school where he would receive instruction for the less prepared boys. Very soon she was visited by "Neighbor Faxon," who warned her that if James continued at the school the other students would drop out. "Pray, Mr. Faxon," Abigail tactfully asked, "has the boy misbehaved?"

"Oh no! That is not the matter," replied the uneasy Faxon. "It was just . . ."

"Well, they don't object to going to church or to dances with James or playing with him," Abigail persisted. "Why should there be objections going to school with him?"

"It is not me who objects," Faxon assured Abigail, "it is the others in the community."

"What others?" Abigail asked sharply. "If it is the 'others' who object, why didn't they come, then?"

The perplexed and helpless Faxon stood before the wife of the president of the United States as she lectured him on the meaning of America:

"This, Mr. Faxon, is attacking the principle of liberty and equality upon the only grounds upon which it ought to be supported, an equality of rights. As a free man James has as much right as any other young man, and a black face should not bar him from school. How do you expect him to prepare himself to earn a living?"

"Oh, ma'am, you are quite right," Faxon conceded, looking toward the door. "I hope you won't take any offense."

"None at all, Mr. Faxon. Only be so good as to send the young man to me. . . . I have not thought it any disgrace to myself to take him into my parlor and teach him both to read and write. Tell them, Mr. Faxon . . . I hope we shall all go to heaven together."

Abigail Adams, the second first lady, and the first who knew that life was more than baking cookies.

5

The French: Foe or Friend?

John Adams was sworn in on March 4, 1797, the son of a humble
Massachusetts farmer inducted into the highest political office of
the land. Often in American history, the period immediately following the president taking office has been called a "honeymoon," a
time when reality is suspended so that illusion may enjoy a few
days of delight. Adams may have had a honeymoon with Abigail,
but not with the world of politics. No sooner had he become president than he had to deal with troubling news from Europe. The
new French government, a five-headed executive committee
known as the Directory, had refused to accept the credentials of
America's minister to France, Charles Pinckney, and ordered him
expelled from the country. France had been upset with the Jay
Treaty, which had America siding with England and breaking the
alliance it had with France during the Revolution. The French had
made significant contributions to America's victory over England,
and the names Rochambeau, Lafayette, and de Grasse had become
part of the legacy of '76, having fought valiantly alongside Washington. Adams, who had lived in Paris for several years, was aware of
French sensibilities, and he had no desire to see America alienated
from its old ally.

Adams decided to send a mission to Paris consisting of Pinckney,
John Marshall, and Elbridge Gerry. The envoys were instructed to
convey messages of friendship and request compensation for French

depredation of American commercial vessels in the Caribbean. The three-man team recorded in complete detail the exchanges with Talleyrand, the French minister of foreign affairs, and his agents, one of whom was a Dutch banker, and the other two who were what we might call today "fund-raisers." One agent took Pinckney into a private room and whispered that he had a message from the Directory. The French government, he relayed, was irritated by a speech President Adams made, but all would be well if Adams softened his future speeches, if America loaned France 22 million Dutch guilders, and if a sum of money, a *pot-de-vin*, or *douceur*, or, to be frank, a bribe, of 50,000 pounds sterling be made available to Talleyrand.

Stunned, perplexed by the proposals, the envoys heard conflicting stories by the agents, whom President Adams would later specify as X, Y, Z. One of them told the Americans that the money to Talleyrand was nothing more than a lawyer's fee for services rendered. But it became clear that only with the money turned over to the French foreign minister would he endeavor to have the Directory receive the Americans. When Talleyrand met personally with the Americans, he put the pressure on, threatening that countries refusing to aid the French government would be regarded as enemies. The Americans grumbled among themselves. "Gentlemen," declared one of the agents, "you do not speak to the point; it is money. It is expected that you will offer money." Pinckney replied that they had addressed that point. "No," charged the agent, "you have not, what is your answer?" A famous rejoinder, usually attributed to Pinckney, which persists in history textbooks, is: "Millions for defence, but not one cent for tribute." But what was actually recorded in the dispatch, sent by the envoys to the secretary of state, reads: "No, no, not a sixpence!"

Insulted by the thought of bribery, the American envoys were perhaps even more concerned over the French demanding that America renounce its Neutrality Proclamation. The Virginian James Monroe, and others on Jefferson's side, informed the Directory that Adams did not represent the views of the American people. Talleyrand and his agents could now resort to intimidation. "Y" delivered a naked threat to the Americans. If no money was forthcoming, France would bring the full force of her power against the United States, and the young republic, no more than two decades old, could suffer the fate of the Venetian republic and disappear from history altogether. Talleyrand, who knew the U.S. Constitution did not authorize envoys to negotiate loans, nonetheless persisted with his threats, claiming the United States deserved "no more consideration than Genoa or Geneva." The American envoys were even warned not to reveal a word of the exchanges to their own government. If they did so in the hope of uniting their country, the effort would collapse. For a superior and sagacious French diplomacy would blame the British party (Federalists) for the collapse of negotiations and do so with the full support of the French party (Republicans).

The American envoys could only express sadness and dismay. America, the only nation on earth that had shown true friendship toward France, now found herself threatened with extinction simply for refusing to cough up money for tribute. Talleyrand, who had no patience for sentimentality, had his agents inform the envoys that he was about to send a letter to their government in which he would report that the commissioners were uncooperative and "unfriendly." Calling Talleyrand's bluff, Pinckney and Marshall departed France and Gerry stayed on in Paris, fearful that war between the two countries might occur if he were not present to prevent it.

Even before hearing of the breakdown of negotiations, Adams's patience with France was wearing thin. While the Republicans continued to praise France, a French privateer, the *Vertitude*, sailed into the harbor of Charleston and sacked and burned a British vessel at anchor, an action that made a mockery of American territorial sovereignty. In the Caribbean, there were said to be sixty to eighty French privateers blocking scores of American vessels. The French government ordered the seizure of American vessels bound to or from Britain or storing British goods on board. In July 1798, one American schooner, the *Sally* of Plymouth, Massachusetts, was overtaken by a French privateer and all of her crew, except the mate, were removed and replaced by seven Frenchmen. A week later the mate, armed with a handspike, killed the French crew one by one, sparing the life of a single young man, and sailed the schooner safely home. News traveled slowly, but the young American republic was a highly literate society, and such stories of exploits on the high seas were widely read and discussed.

When news arrived of the XYZ debacle, two members of Adams's cabinet advised him to ask Congress for a declaration of war. Adams, convinced that war was inevitable, wrote down thoughts about America's misplaced faith in the French Revolution. The heresy America has lived with, he noted, is the "false" and "dishonorable" conviction that the principles of the two revolutions are one and the same. "Ours was resistance to innovation, theirs was innovation itself, which we have no right to censure or applaud." But Adams recognized that the country was far from prepared, materially and mentally, for a war, and that the Republicans would resist it. Rumors were rife in Congress about the negotiations, and the president was requested to supply the dispatches. When he responded and made his speech to Congress, on April 3, 1798, he delivered a bombshell. Although Adams gave a restrained address, Congress was outraged and the country was shocked to learn that the French demanded bribes with implied threats and insults to the nation's honor. Even the pro-French Republicans were totally unprepared for what a historian has aptly called "this hard evidence of Gallic perfidy."

Jefferson, however, termed Adams's address an "insane message," and he insisted that Adams was exaggerating the XYZ affair to discredit the French Revolution (which had already, it would seem, discredited itself under Robespierre's reign of terror). But the country rallied to Adams, who became an instant national hero, and for the first and only time he was the idol of his party. The executive office was flooded with petitions supporting the president. State militias were formed as symbolic expressions of national defense, and thousands of dollars were collected to start building a navy. Anti-French reaction affected Americans from all walks of life: artisans, farmers, merchants, mechanics, women, children, and young men, who volunteered their services to the army. Recalling the Citizen Genet affair under the Washington administration, people thought that France was once again trying to interfere in America's domestic politics and divide the country. The behavior of France came as a shock since she had once been at the side of America in time of direst need. But the XYZ episode seemed proof that France had lost her way. "She once fought for liberty," announced the Massachusetts legislature; "she now contends for domination."

ADAMS VERSUS TALLEYRAND

"The whole of Adams's single term," the historians Stanley Elkins and Eric McKitrick have written, "was absorbed, to a degree unequaled in any other presidency, with a single problem, a crisis in foreign relations." It could also be said that the whole of Adams's political philosophy had been absorbed, to a degree unequal in any other president, with theories of civil government that dealt with a single problem, avoiding a crisis in social relations between the classes. One might think that Adams's early writings poorly prepared him to face the field of international relations, a world in which a government deals not with its own citizens but with other nations. On the contrary, Adams's writings and reflections more than adequately prepared him to handle foreign relations, and for several reasons.

First, Adams's thoughts on government inevitably dealt with the phenomenon of human nature and the causes and motives of human action. The emotions of rivalry, envy, jealousy, revenge, pride, and the demand for recognition may be even stronger in diplomatic relations than in human relations. "Can you discover the Cause of the great Balance of exchange in favor of England?" Adams asked Jefferson in 1785, suggesting that out of resentment of having lost the colonies England was flooding the market with goods and harassing America's merchant vessels. "They grudge to every other people, a single ship and a single seaman. The consequence of this Envy, in the end, will be the loss of all their own. They seem at present to dread American ships and seamen more than any other. Their Jealousy of our navigation is so strong" that they risk bankruptcy with their revengeful tactics. Whether in domestic politics or diplomatic relations, human action is driven by the same motives, and Adams was rarely at a loss in grasping the causes of events.

A second reason Adams's early writings prepared him for the challenge of diplomacy is that they dealt with the phenomenon of power. Adams would hardly be surprised to find out that the international world of politics is unresponsive to reason and good intentions. "Power naturally grows," he wrote in *Discourses on Davila*. "Why? Because human passions are insatiable." Passion itself is driven by desire, which may explain behavior but cannot control it. Thus power has its own purposes: to expand, augment, dominate, and control. Power, like liberty, is neither benign nor bad in itself; it is to be judged by how it is used, whether for good or ill. Adams believed that the "essence of free government is the effective control of rivalries," by which he meant, the control of *rivalries by rivalries*. So too would the essence of enlightened diplomacy be the effective control of contending nation-states in activities beyond their borders in a world of power politics. Not that Adams was advocating an interventionist foreign policy. But he did recognize that "the weaker will ever be the lamb in the paws of the wolfe." In the Revolution America was the lamb and England the wolf, and the colonies turned to France for support, looking to a monarchist regime to defeat a parliamentary government.

Adams's belief in the vital role of the executive office to establish an equilibrium between democracy and aristocracy, between the "credulous many" and the "artful few," is not too unlike the balance of power theory later developed by Otto von Bismarck. The German chancellor believed that power operates in ways that can be made stable if seen not as a clash of dualities but of tri-polarities. So conceived, one's own country finds its strength not by aligning with one nation-state against another but instead by maintaining a careful stance between the two so that power is balanced and checked by its own situation of counterpoise. Curiously, Adams's heir Henry Adams looked to science in the late nineteenth century and saw the phenomenon of entropy and the second law of thermodynamics that spelled chaos and disorder in the universe. But President Adams was closer to the physicist Isaac Newton and the philosopher James Harrington in seeing the possibilities of statics, the theory of juxtaposed forces and equilibrium. "There can be, in the nature of things, no balance without three powers," observed

Adams, and in politics as in nature the existence of only two powers meant that one will eventually "swallow up" the other. Similarly, international relations dealing with power blocs requires the presence of a third mediating force to achieve a kind of triangular equipoise. Steeped in Alexander Pope's insight that conflicting passions cannot be gotten rid of but only countervailed against one another, Adams also anticipated Bismarck's view that a country can enjoy power by engaging in a policy of nonalignment. "However we may consider ourselves," he stated in his message to Congress in May 1797, "the maritime and commercial powers of the world will consider the United States of America as forming a weight in the balance of power in Europe, which never can be forgotten or neglected. It would not only be against our interest, but it would be doing wrong to one half of Europe at least, if we should voluntarily throw ourselves into either scale."

But Talleyrand, it will be recalled, ridiculed the idea that America could enter the modern world of realpolitik, and when he likened America to Geneva, he was dismissing the young republic as small, weak, isolated, with no knowledge of how power works— or how money speaks!

Talleyrand may have been surprised to discover that America could not be bribed or intimidated. The confrontation between Talleyrand and Adams could well suggest the difference between a slouching Catholic and a strait Puritan; between one who believes that sin condemns the sinner to corruption and one who believes that sin is there to be resisted. Charles-Maurice de Talleyrand-Périgord had spent two years in America, where he had ingratiated himself with leading political figures and invested in speculative land ventures. A renegade bishop who walked with a limp from a childhood injury, Talleyrand sported a flowing wig and dandyish silk coats. He and Adams did share one thing in common, the conviction that diplomacy operates best behind closed doors and that discretion is the better part of virtue. Although the French Revolution was made in the name of "liberty, equality, and fraternity," the diplomacy carried on by the Directory had more to do with secrecy, bureaucracy, and fait accompli. But the two figures had strikingly different careers as well as characters. While Adams proved incapable of continuing for a second term in office, Talleyrand seemed to continue forever. He was a survivor; having been present at the outbreak of the French Revolution and having escaped the Terror, he served under Napoleon Bonaparte and, upon his overthrow, the Bourbon restoration of 1815 and again under Louis-Phillipe in 1830.

Talleyrand presents the world of international relations with a quandary: a diplomat who serves his country for his own personal purposes, a man of moral weakness and political wisdom, one "unable to resist," as the Dutch historian Pieter Geyl put it, "the temptation to line his pockets and yet have clear-sighted and sound ideas about international politics and about the hollowness of wars of conquest." To this day historians are unsure whether Talleyrand used his office for his own interests or allowed the Directory to use him for its own purposes. Probably both.

The American public, of course, saw the XYZ affair from their own perspective and, as John Quincy Adams later observed, they misinterpreted the intentions of Talleyrand, who was actually sympathetic to America and saw President Adams as more conciliatory toward France than Washington had been. Talleyrand and his agents, having investments in America, had a vested interest in maintaining peace with the United States. They saw themselves as a reliable intermediary between America and the Directory. Talleyrand did manage to gain the Directory's approval to halt piracy in the West Indies. Often acting on his own, he sought to restore the professional standards of the French diplomatic corps, still reeling from the bloody purges of 1791 to 1795.

Talleyrand and his agents also appreciated John Adams as possibly more accommodating to the French. Was there a contradiction in Adams's desire for peace and his belligerent speech to Congress, where he had accused the Directory of "searching to propagate anarchy and division in the United States"? The Directory may have been offended, but Talleyrand knew Adams's speech was delivered only to satisfy the pro-English Federalists. Although the French government had supported Jefferson in the election of 1796, and although French thinkers knew of Adams's hostility to the French Revolution, the Directory refrained from interfering in American politics and did not, as was commonly believed, work with the Jeffersonian Republicans to undermine the administration. Talleyrand even recommended to the Directory that it enter into formal negotiations with Adams and his young republic.

Thus history presents us with two Talleyrands. One was, out front, all bribe and bluff, charming, deceitful, one given to threats and ultimatums. The other was, behind the scenes, all cunning and conceit, one playing by the rules, more interested in results than insults. Will we ever know whether Talleyrand was America's true friend or jealous enemy? We do know from his memoirs that he begrudgingly paid America a compliment. The colonies in the New World, he wrote, knew how to start a revolution, how to fight it, how to win it, and—something France could not do—how to end it.

Adams desired to respond to Talleyrand's overture for negotiation, but pressures from his own anti-French Federalist Party led him to proceed cautiously. Earlier, when sending over three envoys to France, Adams sought to appoint Jefferson, who refused to be part of the mission; then he tried to have at least one Republican, and again he was unsuccessful. Thus his effort to build a consensus behind American diplomacy succumbed to partisan politics, even within his own cabinet. Neither the Republicans nor his own Federalists would support the president's efforts at bipartisan diplomacy.

HAMILTON AND THE ARCH-FEDERALISTS

Although Adams wisely chose to avoid a war with France, a political war was taking place on the streets of American cities. In Philadelphia, the capital, a brawl broke out between two gangs, one wearing the French tricolor cockade, the other the black cockade resembling those worn by Washington's troops. The cavalry had to be brought in to separate the pro- and anti-French factions. Suspicion and hatred were everywhere. The house of Benjamin Franklin Bache, Franklin's grandson and editor of the Republican *Aurora*, was trashed and left without doors and windows. Rumors spread that French agents would set fire to the city, which had to be patrolled all night long. Adams allowed a guard to be posted before the president's house.

The Republicans regarded the XYZ affair as a red herring, a crisis deliberately manufactured abroad to strengthen Adams's position at home. How do we know, they charged, that the administration did not misrepresent the views of Talleryrand and his emissaries? France is a "sister republic," and the administration was antagonizing the Directory to provoke it into declaring war on the United States. Citing a parallel case, Jefferson exculpated the Directory. "When the Portuguese Ambassador yielded to like attempts at swindlers, the conduct of the Directory in imprisoning him for an attempt at corruption, as well as their general conduct, really magnanimous, places them above suspicion."

The Republicans made every effort to frustrate attempts at military preparation. The Washington administration had passed an executive order prohibiting arming merchant ships in peacetime, and Adams asked Congress to repeal the ban. Jefferson stood opposed, and he also insisted that any executive order removing the ban would be unconstitutional. France's true enemy was England, not America, exhorted Vice President Jefferson. To Adams's dismay, much of the public supported Jefferson's opposition to any efforts at self-defense. But Adams was able to persuade Congress to build the forty-four-gun frigate the *United States,* the pride and joy of the president, who had always dreamed of "wooden walls" as a fortress for the country. Congress also passed a bill providing for a navy of twelve vessels, but his request for a real fleet was turned down and a provision for a regular army of twenty-five thousand men was amended and reduced to ten thousand.

In the theory of classical republicanism, a standing army posed a threat to liberty, and the Republicans could only suspect the Federalist support of such measures as further evidence of aristocratic and monarchical tendencies. The specter of a standing army conjured up images of the scum of the streets armed to the teeth and led by an elite corps of officers. With such an image of a European *canaille* in mind, Jefferson opposed both a standing army and a sustained navy, and had he had his way, America would later have found itself in the War of 1812 with neither.

"My entrance into office is marked by a misunderstanding with France, which I shall endeavor to reconcile," John Adams wrote to his son at the outset of his administration, but not if it means "too much humiliation," he added. The son, John Quincy Adams, though young, would have been the ideal diplomatic envoy to send to Paris with the other envoys. But Adams was too sensitive to the charge of nepotism to make the appointment, and with the disastrous failure of the first mission, the president needed a new approach to the French Directory, whose murky purposes defied clear interpretation.

America's relations with France during Adams's administration came to be called the Quasi War. Both sides were poised in armed opposition, with France acting aggressively against American merchant vessels and America preparing for a military showdown. France, still owed money from loans to America to fight England, asserted the right to prey upon American ships and confiscate their cargoes and impress their men since America had made a treaty with England, her enemy. Republicans, enjoying a majority in the House, were reluctant to give Adams a full naval force to protect American commerce in the Caribbean. Still, the *Constitution* and several other frigates, armed with the latest firepower and sailing technology, performed well during the Quasi War and managed to destroy a few French fighting ships, to the surprise of the world.

The possibility of war seldom unifies a country until war breaks out. During the Adams administration, America found itself bitterly divided. Led by Jefferson, Republicans believed a war with France would drive America into the arms of England, where they suspected Adams sought to take America, the better to cultivate his alleged aristo-monocratic tendencies. Britain, with her powerful navy, ruled the seas, and thus, reasoned the Republicans, she represented a greater threat to American commerce and freedom.

The difference between Adams's Federalists and Jefferson's Republicans was as much economic as ideological. The northern Federalists had financial ties with England, where some American families were related to members in the British treasury and Hamilton eagerly sought the support of London bankers. The South also traded with England, where planters sold their tobacco, rice, and other products, much of which was marketed in Europe. England also supplied planters with imported goods and loans. Thus, the

South found itself in the very place where it had been before the Revolution, once again indebted to London merchants and looking upon England not only as a nation of shopkeepers but of avaricious bankers and creditors. The charge of British influence resonated throughout the South, and the Republicans exploited it.

But even in Adams's own Federalist Party there was no unanimity on matters of diplomacy. The extreme elements, called "arch-Federalists," were passionately anti-French and pro-British. Adams's secretary of state, Pickering, would mount an ideological crusade against the menace of Jacobinism, with its infidelity and anarchy, and to do so he would have America make common cause with England. Another arch-Federalist, George Cabot, senator from Massachusetts, feared that Adams would become a tool of Jefferson and allow his thoughts to be persuaded by the Francophiles. The arch-Federalists had suspected Adams as soft from the moment he made his conciliatory inaugural address. Most extreme was William Cobbett, the British controversialist temporarily in residence in the United States while editing his journal *The Porcupine Gazette.* Cobbett attacked fellow English exile Tom Paine, warned against a French invasion to America assisted by a conspiracy of Irish immigrants, called black Americans "Samboes," spent time in jail for wife beating, and somehow managed to get himself invited to dine with the president and first lady. More influential was Fisher Ames, the Massachusetts congressman who distrusted democracy and its populist impulses, feared the Constitution as a fragile structure, doubted that the republic would survive into the nineteenth century, and agreed with Hamilton that "your people, sir, is a great beast!"

Although Hamilton was anti-French and pro-British, he was not a war hawk. Adams listened to his unwarlike secretary of war, McHenry, who in turn proffered Hamilton's advice that the country and its representatives were not ready for a declaration of war. But Hamilton had come out of political retirement and he reentered the stage of national affairs with the aim of having the government create a full-fledged army. Who would lead it? Hamilton had been in communication with Washington, advising him that in the event of an "open rupture" with France, the people would turn to the general to once again lead America to victory. Washington, however, doubted that the situation was that grave, and he implicitly declined the invitation to head the army. Pickering wanted to see Hamilton to take command of the proposed army and asked Washington to recommend him. But the general reminded the cabinet secretary that the decision was up to the president of the United States. Washington did submit three recommendations, with Hamilton second in command, and the first position left to Adams to decide. Then Adams departed for Quincy without making any appointments.

His departure implicitly left decision making in the hands of the cabinet, who favored Hamilton. Hamilton could now have his army. The situation was humiliating to Adams, the country's commander in chief, kept out of vital military decisions. Adams did not deny Hamilton's talents as a military leader. But why, he and others wondered, did Hamilton want his army? Would not such a creation make war with France inevitable? Some Federalists were upset that the Republican Elbridge Gerry still remained in France communicating with Talleyrand; others sounded warnings of a French invasion. Adams, no longer the hero of the hour as he had been with the XYZ affair, seemed disgruntled and detached, sulking away his time at Quincy. When McHenry urged him to return to Washington, Adams cited his wife's ill health as the reason for remaining. He added ominously that the raising of army regiments was costly and without any apparent purpose. "At present there is no more prospect of seeing a French army here, than there is in Heaven."

John Adams was much beloved in his home state of Massachusetts, where he had a reputation as standing as solid as New England granite in the coming of the Revolution. People knew he would never wobble when facing the apparent duplicity of the French or the jealousy of the English. John and Abigail were deeply touched by the cheering crowds lining the streets in Boston. But in other parts of the country, and particularly in Philadelphia, sentiment was unpredictable and even cruel. Bache's *Aurora* published Talleyrand's version of the XYZ affair to claim that Adams had distorted the nature of the negotiations, and the president was described as "old, querulous, bald, blind, crippled, toothless Adams." The attacks on her husband outraged Abigail. Some Federalists, arguing that the opposition had gone too far in distorting the news and undermining the integrity of government, bristled at the attacks in the presss. "Nothing will have an effect until Congress passes a sedition bill," Abigail noted. "The wrath of the Republic ought to fall upon devoted heads," she declared in reference to rabid Republican editors. To Jefferson, the press, at least that which reflected his views, could do no wrong. "If these papers fail," Jefferson wrote to Madison, "republicanism will be entirely browbeaten."

Jefferson once observed that between a country having a government without a press, and one having a press without a government, he would choose the latter. The press along with the party was his means of bringing down government, and he would return government to the people once he himself became the government. What he would do as president could only be what the people wanted and needed him to do. While Adams questioned whether any leader or institution could represent the people as a whole, since they are divided among themselves, Jefferson saw democracy as unifying and harmonious. Thus, if Adams may have sulked in a fit of doubt and self-interrogation, Jefferson could only enjoy the confidence of self-legitimization. But the author of the *Federalist* and the author of the *Defence* both believed that only a carefully devised constitution could control the "passions" and "interests" of a divided people. Jefferson, in contrast, saw the people as essentially rational and good and at one with themselves. The "chosen people of God" lacked not virtue but a voice.

6

War Measures, Free Speech, States' Rights

THE ALIEN AND SEDITION ACTS

Summer 1798 represented both the pinnacle of the Adams administration and its abrupt decline. The XYZ affair had made Adams a hero in the eyes of the country, and the Republican opposition found itself on the defensive. Congress was in a mood to give Adams whatever he asked for, even approving the establishment of a Department of Navy, headed by the able Benjamin Stoddard, who directed the construction of armed vessels authorized to attack any French craft threatening American commerce. But with the Republicans in retreat, Congress also gave Adams what the first lady had been asking for but the president himself did not eagerly want, a notorious batch of laws that became, for reasons of party politics, an offer he could not refuse—the Alien and Sedition Acts.

In American history, almost every important presidency has had its one moment of deep regret, an action taken that might have been avoided, one that backfired and played into the hands of the opposition. Presidential memoirs are strewn with apologetics or even denials that the executive office had anything to do with what turned out to be a political disaster. In this instance, even "honest" John Adams said of the Alien and Sedition Acts that they had little to do with his program and that he had "recommended no such thing." Some historians insist that Adams had no record of "complicity in framing the acts" and that he had earlier defended free speech in the context of radical Whig ideology in America's struggle with England. Other historians, noting how Adams complained of press attacks on the presidency as "libelous," and even came close to calling Francophiles "traitorous," believed he helped shape the climate of opinion that produced the infamous legislation.

The acts, passed by Congress and signed into law by Adams, comprised four laws. The Naturalization Act attempted to curtail the flow of aliens admitted to the country by extending the residency requirement for citizenship from five to fourteen years. The legislation registered not only jitters about a possible war with France but the presence of political refugees in the United States. Some Frenchmen and -women were from Paris or Santo Domingo and brought with them the lingering sentiments of the Girondins, Jacobins, or Royalists. Others were from England, like the secular scientist Joseph Priestley, who "joining chemic with religion's hate, try'd to decompose church and state," or the scandalmonger J. Thomas Callender, the "foul-penned journalist" who started the story, perhaps true, about Thomas Jefferson and his alleged young black mistress Sally Hemings. Like the "horse jockey" whom Adams encountered in Quincy, many fugitives felt as free as a wildman in postrevolutionary America, ready to attack all symbols of authority without fear of guillotine, ax, noose, Bastille, Tower, or Court.

The French revolutionary Directory went all out to persuade Ireland that America had set the example of how to break away from the British Empire. To escape oppressive British rule and the hardships of rural life, many Irish immigrants flocked to America not necessarily as devout Catholics but as radical Republicans sympathetic to France. One earlier arrival was the scrappy, boisterous Matthew Lyon, who came to America as an indentured servant, fought in the Revolution, and went on to become wealthy in land speculation and a Republican congressman from Vermont. When Roger Griswold of Connecticut made a slur upon the Vermonter's military record, Lyon rose from his seat and spat in his face. A House committee voted not to expel "Spitting Matt," and days later Griswold approached Lyon and struck him repeatedly with a heavy hickory walking stick. Lyon fled to the front of the hall and seized a set of fireplace tongs and the two went at it with fists, wood, and steel. The Speaker refused to call the House to order as the congressmen swung at each other and rolled on the floor until the bloodied two were separated. In Philadelphia, the fight was the talk of the town. Abigail complained of the "beastly transported Lyon," that "wild Irishman" allowed to keep his seat in the House presided over by men not courageous enough "to expel the wretch." Lyon came to the New World as a Francophile who would do everything to save America from the English. Of this rabid Republican, John Adams must have thought (as did Brendan Behan, the twentieth-century playright disillusioned with IRA terrorists): "Who'll save Ireland from the Irish?"

The Naturalization Act, aimed at discouraging the arrival of political fugitives at a time when America was in an undeclared naval war with France, had no constitutional implications, even though the measure did imply that political opposition organized by refugees could pose a threat of treason to the republic. Far more controversial on legal grounds were the Alien Act, the Alien Enemies Act, and the Sedition Act. The first authorized the president to order the expulsion of aliens judged dangerous to the peace and safety of the country. The second allowed the president, in the event of war, to order the deportation of aliens of an enemy country or to subject those remaining in the country to restraints on their freedoms. The third, the most controversial Sedition Act, made it a serious misdemeanor, subject to a fine of not more than $5,000 and imprisonment for not more than five years, for anyone to obstruct the operations of a U.S. law. Even more potentially repressive, the act made it illegal for any person to write, print, or publish "any false, scandalous and malicious writing . . . against the government of the United States, or either house of the Congress . . . or the President . . . with the intent to defame . . . or bring them, or either of them, into contempt or disrepute; or to excite against them, or either or any of them, the hatred of the good people of the United States."

Abigail was ecstatic. With such acts America could now rid the country of rabble-rousers like Matthew Lyon, "the Beast of Vermont." Like future first ladies, Abigail waged a campaign against the press that had been attacking her husband. "Let the vipers cease to hiss," she exclaimed. "They will be destroyed with their own poison." She sent her sister a specimen of the journalistic assaults, "the daring outrage which called for the Arm of Government." The politics of the 1790s could turn the gentlest soul into a Lady Macbeth.

As for President Adams himself, he did sign warrants for the deportations of John Burke, editor of the *New York Time Piece*, and William Duane, editor of the *Philadelphia Aurora*—both on Abigail's hit list. But the warrants were never carried out. Adams, who played no role in framing the bill or introducing it to Congress, approved of its passage, but his heart was not in it—unlike the arch-Federalist secretary of state Pickering, who was busy working out a strategy for shutting down the opposition press. With the unseating of the Federalists in the election of 1800, the acts expired at the end of their two-year limit, without a single alien deported.

"THE SOUL OF SOVEREIGNTY IS WOUNDED"

Did the Sedition Act violate the Constitution, especially the First Amendment, where it is specified that Congress shall make no law "abridging" freedom of speech, press, and assembly? Adams insisted, as would Abraham Lincoln during the secession crisis that precipitated the Civil War in 1861, that a government comes into being to guarantee the self-preservation of the people, which it can do only by protecting itself as well as its citizens, and that guarantee could well be jeopardized by those who would subvert the republic. It has been estimated that at the time there were as many as thirty thousand Frenchmen in America, as well as thousands of Englishmen and Irishmen, all refugees from their own countries. No doubt many would prove loyal to America and its political institutions, but many sympathized with revolutionary France. Indeed, the very threat of an alien bill so alarmed French agents in the country that, according to Jefferson, they arranged for a ship to take back to Paris the disgruntled and desperate, who finally realized that the American people were not about to rise up against their government to please the Directory.

Still, the constitutional issues stuck like a thorn in the heart of the Adams administration, especially in light of a president who revered the rule of law. In formulating the bill, Federalists in Congress drew upon the English tradition of common law, where there would be "no prior restraint" of freedom of expression before publication but possible seditious utterances could be prosecuted afterward. Indeed, America's act turned out to be milder than the common law, which did not require proof of intent to commit subversion or insurrection; publication itself was incriminatory. The American law allowed the establishing of the truth of a libelous sentiment to be considered, not merely the expression of opinion but its content and motive, and it could be up to the jury to determine the case.

The Sedition Act has divided historians of our era as much as it bitterly divided partisan factions in the late eighteenth century. Stanley Elkins and Eric McKitrick believe Adams's opponents were interpreting the Constitution so strictly for ideological reasons, to deny the president the ability to function in situations of urgency. The opposition displayed a "willingness to renounce a range of positive opportunities for action in return for principle which will inhibit government for undertaking a range of things one does not approve." At issue was not legal scruple but politics as usual. Similarly, David McCullough agrees with Adams himself that the Alien and Sedition Acts are to be regarded as "war measures," and they should be remembered as such, particularly in an era of fear and insecurity. Page Smith also reminds us that the struggle between the Federalists and Republicans represented a war itself, a battle of tongue and pen, spleen and slander. Of the opposition press that Adams had to contend with, it was, Smith writes, "perhaps the most violent and virulent that was to appear in a century and a half of American history."

Republicans, of course, saw things differently. In June 1798, Albert Gallatin, an advisor to Jefferson, rose before his fellow congressmen to explain what the Federalists were attempting to do—shift power from the periphery to the center, from the states to the federal government. All governments enjoy the right of self-preservation, Gallatin acknowledged, but laws ruling on the status of aliens and that of free speech belong to the respective states. Gallatin and other Republicans drew a distinction between national and domestic affairs, between, on the one hand, international commerce and wars

and defense, and, on the other, such internal issues as taxes and western land distribution. On domestic matters, the Constitution must be
interpreted strictly and the president's authority curtailed; only in
international affairs can the power of the federal government be
interpreted broadly. Obviously, the Republicans did not regard the
Alien and Sedition Acts as "war measures," as did Adams; instead,
they involved the issues of free speech, whose jurisdiction belonged
to the states alone and not the national government.

But beyond the theoretical niceties remained the realities of politics. The Republicans accused the Federalists of doing what later
historians accused the Republicans of doing—using the fears gener-
ated by the Quasi War for political purposes. Gallatin claimed that
the Sedition bill "must be considered only as a weapon used by a
party now in power," a means of attacking civil liberties as the first
step in destroying the republic and turning America into a monarchy. Similarly, the Federalists believed that opposition to the acts
came from those who would make America hospitable to a "precious horde of San Culotte cut-throats," the street guerrillas of the
French Revolution.

Ultimately at stake was not only partisan politics but a deeper
issue that would not be resolved until it was decided on the bloody
battlefields of the Civil War: Where does sovereignty lay? Responding vehemently to the Alien and Sedition Acts, James Madison and
Thomas Jefferson arranged for the states of Kentucky and Virginia
to issue resolutions declaring the right to negate and void acts of
Congress deemed unconstitutional. The Sedition Act, announced
the Virginia Resolutions of 1799, was "the offspring of . . . tremen-
dous pretensions, which inflict a death-wound on the Sovereignty
of the States." The opposition to Adams, then, was not arguing the
case for free speech and press as much as states' rights, the authority of the state to judge what is to be considered seditious and
libelous.

Such a stance could be seen as an embarrassment to Madison,
who, in the earlier debates over the Constitution in 1787, took the
exact opposite position, insisting that the federal government had
the right to null and void acts of state legislatures. Nor would Jefferson be able to make up his mind where sovereignty ultimately

resided. Before he became president, sovereignty would lie in the states; afterward, in the federal government, now presided over by one who would proceed, without constitutional authority, to purchase the Louisiana Territory and impose an embargo on free trade. But in the heated controversies surrounding the Adams administration, theoretical consistency succumbs to party politics without so much as a blush.

The debates over the Alien and Sedition Acts go to the foundations of American political philosophy. Adams and the Federalists believed that a strong government with checks and balances is the best guarantee of liberty. Jefferson and the Republicans believed that the best guarantee of liberty lies with the states and their closer proximity to the people, and people need fewer checks and balances, certainly not virtuous, self-governing Americans.

Contemporary historians of a Jeffersonian bent have embellished the Republican argument. The Alien and Sedition Acts, writes Peter S. Onuf and Leonard J. Sadosky, is further evidence that "both the executive and legislative power had fallen into the hands of forces inimical to the republican experiment," for the acts allowed "no protected space within which the perfect republic could be preserved." Another historian, Richard Rosenfeld, charges that the Adams administration was the worst ever to happen in American political history, one that left the country on the verge of war and liberty strangled to death by the Alien and Sedition Acts that brought about an "era of terror."

"*Terror!*" The specific term arose from the French Revolution that was taking place across the Atlantic, the very event that the Republicans defended and that, one should remember, left a bloody trail of beheaded corpses in baskets, all guillotined in the name of popular sovereignty, "*la volonte souveraine du peuple,*" the very shibboleth Jefferson extolled. Even more difficult to accept is the thesis that the acts of the Adams administration left no "protected space" for the republic to survive. After all, during the "era of terror" the courts continued to function, trial by jury still remained an option, the separation of powers kept its bearings, the press published without restraint or abridgment, democratic politics went about its

usual ways, aliens were alive and well, most home-grown sedition-
ists went free (with the exceptions of Callender and Lyon, who did
time in the slammer, and a thirty-day jail sentence to Abijah Adams,
no relation), and elections were held on schedule and even saw the
defeat of the Federalist Party. A regime that was supposedly undermining the republic in order to bring back monarchy is hardly a
regime that would relinquish power without putting up an extra-
political struggle—instead of going out of office without a bang or a
whimper, with neither a terror nor a tear.

NULLIFICATION AND NATIONALISM

If the Alien and Sedition Acts backfired, since they became unpop-
ular and did nothing to unify the country and served only to create
martyrs, so too did Jefferson's and Madison's Virginia and Kentucky
resolutions. But there was a difference. The acts of the Federalist
Congress were immediately identified with the Adams administration, whereas almost no one knew of the origins of the state resolutions, who was behind them and for what ends. Jefferson acted in
complete secrecy, arranging local assembly members in Kentucky
to front for his designs while agents in the Republican Party created
the impression that the resolutions were truly democratic and represented the spontaneous sentiments of the people. The resolutions
were the first articulation of what came to be known as the doctrine of nullification: the right of a state to declare its sovereignty by
judging for itself whether the federal government's exercise of
power is undelegated and therefore "unauthoritative, void, and of
no force."

Jefferson, one who had a penchant for propinquity, a conviction
that what is near is precious and what is far is treacherous, expected
that nullification would arouse public excitement throughout the
country and bring national support to the southern-based Republican Party. But the states adjoining Kentucky and Virginia remained
indifferent and refused to endorse the resolutions, and in Pennsylvania and New York, where Republican sentiment had been strong,
little opposition to the Alien and Sedition Acts had expressed itself.

If Adams overestimated the possible seeds of sedition in America, Jefferson underestimated the stronger sentiment of nationalism.

Abigail Adams denounced "the mad resolutions of Virginia and Kentucky." Did she or her husband know that Jefferson was behind them? America's own vice president had concocted a formula for the dissolution of the republic. Had America known that Jefferson was a closet secessionist, he may have not had a political future. Alexander Hamilton, Jefferson's archenemy, had no immediate knowledge of the background of the resolutions, but he had little doubt about Jefferson's stealth in the art of political management. Hamilton had opposed the Alien and Sedition Acts as politically unwise, but he remained steadfast in his hostility toward France and he made clear his intention to hold the administration to his views on foreign policy. Adams, however, was not one to be intimidated, even by a character as strong-willed as Hamilton.

Among the Federalists, America's relations with France were strained due to the role of Elbridge Gerry, the former Massachusetts representative who had voted against some Hamiltonian measures and could not be trusted by the party. To the consternation of the arch-Federalists, Gerry stayed on in Paris and held out hope for a meeting of minds with Talleyrand, and in that hope he first had the support of John Quincy Adams, who assured his father that France had no intention of declaring war on the United States. But back home the impression was that Talleyrand had been manipulating Gerry. "That vile intriguer Talleyrand," Abigail wrote to her son-in-law William Smith, "I fear has entrapped him whom I should have supposed the most wary; like the serpent, he has charmed him, and like him, he will destroy his prey." Gerry's heart may be in the right place, but, poor sap, he "always had a wrong kink in his head."

When Gerry returned from France, on October 1, 1798, in the midst of the bitter debate over the Alien and Sedition Acts, he was met with widespread denunciation by the Boston Federalists, who suspected him of dividing the American commission in France in order to negotiate unilaterally to the detriment of the country's national interests. Still, when Gerry rode out to Quincy to confer with the president, he found Adams receptive to listening to his version of his dealings with Talleyrand. But the president became the butt of criticisms from all sides. The opposition paper *Aurora* accused Adams of creating and sustaining the crisis with France by continuing to exploit the XYZ affair, while praising Gerry as a "prophet of peace" who was advising that it was better to "indemnify" France than to "fight her now and pay her hereafter." Adams himself preferred to buy peace rather than pay for war, but his party was outraged. Secretary Pickering shouted "Shame," and ambassadors in Europe depicted Gerry as arrogant in taking upon himself the responsibility of negotiating, and his accounts of his discussions with Talleyrand were dismissed as unreliable. John Quincy Adams, who sought stable relations with France, also had his doubts, informing his father that the French had in Gerry "a man to deal with who fears a rupture more than dishonor" and, hence, they can drive him to accept any terms, even those unacceptable at home, all the better to foment divisions in America. Adams listened closely to all sides, careful to disassociate sound policy decisions from personality quirks and political passions. But leaders in the Federalist Party remained stubborn, adhering to their earlier hostile and suspicious views of the French, and as the war crisis escalated in winter 1798, Adams appeared maddenly indecisive, pleasing no one but himself, a president who believed firmly in weighing options and acting alone from a position of independence.

"UNITED WE STAND, DIVIDED WE FALL"

While foreign affairs divided the Federalist Party, domestic politics left the Republican Party even more divided and far more frustrated. Perhaps even more than the Alien and Sedition Acts, Jefferson's notion of nullification seemed as dubious as it was divisive, especially since the Virginian had no consistent theoretical foundation on which to articulate the case other than the politics of the moment. Abigail Adams was not the only one to be perplexed at the behavior of Jefferson after he became president, now that he was augmenting the authority of the executive branch, the very office that Adams had once upheld and against which Jefferson had inveighed. At the end of his first term, Jefferson wrote Abigail and proudly told her how he had used the powers of the presidency to negate any remaining sedition law, "because I considered, and now consider, that the law to be a nullity, as absolute and as palpable as if Congress had ordered us to fall down and worship a golden image; and that it was my duty to arrest its execution in every stage as it would have been to rescue from the fiery furnace those who should have been cast into it for refusing to worship the image."

Jefferson saw himself as a rescuer, and he would save America from the Federalists, a party that had as a president a downright "monocrat." Doubtless Abigail knew her husband better than Jefferson did, and she would carry on a correspondence with Jefferson while he was president and afterward, trying to clarify matters, wondering how one man could be so suspicious of another, her own husband who was as harmless as a trusting prince. But Jefferson remains the "American Sphinx," to use Joseph J. Ellis's apt categorization, a politician whose political philosophy defies reason. He sought to preserve the pure integrity of the American republic, but his shifting positions on the notion of sovereignty could easily undermine it.

During the Washington and Adams administrations, Jefferson held that the Supreme Court, no less than the state legislators, had the right to nullify acts of Congress and those of the executive. During his own administration, however, when decrees of the judiciary were at stake, he was for nullification by Congress and the executive. His rationale was that any sentiments and actions he disfavored must, wherever they emanated, come from minority-class rule, to be nullified by any means whatsoever. Thus, for Jefferson, sovereignty could lie in either Congress, the Supreme Court, or the respective states. Yet in republican theory, Parliament or Congress is the supreme seat of authority, and its decisions are uncontestable, unimpeachable, and irresistible. Adams well knew that Congress could go awry, but he also insisted that the definition of a republic is "the rule of law and not of men," and that it is "*consent alone* that makes any human Laws binding." Congress passed the Alien and Sedition Acts, albeit by a narrow margin, and thus they enjoyed the consent of the governed. Adams was aware of the dilemma at the heart of Jeffersonianism, the tension between natural right and popular sovereignty, between the right of individuals to exercise free speech and the right of the elected representative branch of government to undertake measures to ensure national security. But Jefferson, rather than wrestling with the issue of right and sovereignty, simply took sovereignty with him wherever he went, as though he owned it personally and had a natural right to it.

Thus, in January 1799, Jefferson headed south in an attempt to sow the seeds of state sovereignty in his home state of Virginia. The state that had passed resolutions condemning the Alien and Sedition Acts would appear to be prepared to listen to the case for nullification and perhaps even dismemberment and secession. But George Washington, under whom Adams served as vice president, deplored the lead that Virginia had assumed in denouncing the federal government. He could not believe that his fellow Virginians would forsake their loyalty to the government they had consented to form in 1787. To his distress, Virginia had been electing to the state assembly candidates who stood against the general government. In despair, Washington urged Patrick Henry to reenter politics and campaign for a seat either in Congress or in the state legislature. The fiery Henry had become a convert to federalism, but he was too old and feeble to take on the strain of a congressional fight, though he did concede to run for the assembly, making his last memorable speech from the front porch of a rustic tavern in Charlottesville in March 1799.

Henry told the crowd that he shared their frustration at seeing powers gravitating toward the central government. He resisted centralization as much as any Virginian, but events had moved history in directions we must accept, he advised, and resentment must not be confused with righteousness. If the people of Virginia felt intolerably oppressed, they still had a right to overturn government, but they must wait until the infringement was serious and uncorrectable by conventional political means. Meanwhile, "United we stand, divided we fall. Let us not split into factions which must destroy the union upon which our existence hangs." If Virginians opposed the federal government, they would have to face Washington himself, who would lead an army against them. Is there an American "who will dare to lift his hand against the father of his country"? "No, you dare not do it; in such a parricidal attempt, the steel would drop from your nerveless arm!"

It was the "spirit of '76" all over again, Virginians siding with New Englanders in common cause. Adams would call upon Henry to join a peace commission to France, but the old hero of '76, the orator who once exclaimed "Give me Liberty or Give me Death!" had to decline for reasons of health. His greatest support for Adams had already been delivered from the platform of a tavern drinking hole. Cheers!

7

The American Landscape

A COUNTRY INVERTEBRATE AND INERT

John Adams's nemeses were not only Jefferson, Paine, and the Republican Francophiles; they also included American geography. The physical conditions of America in the late 1790s could not help but cling to localism over nationalism. Although America had a Constitution that was supposed to unite the country, the country itself was invertebrate, a body politic without a spinal cord, a loose system without a strong, centralized structure. Americans wanted it that way.

At the Constitutional Convention in 1787, it was assumed that the legislative branch of government "ought to be the most exact transcript of the whole Society," and since society as a whole consisted in the value and significance of its diverse parts, power must be dispersed and sovereignty fragmented. At the very time the framers were drafting the Constitution in Philadelphia, John Adams was in London writing three volumes of political philosophy in defense of it. But whereas the framers were busy working out schemes to allocate certain powers to the federal government while reserving the rest for the states, Adams alone was making the case for the importance of the executive branch of government, the office of the presidency as the one institution that could bring unity and coherence to the country. Most of the Constitution's framers, however, feared the executive, regarding it as a potential source of tyranny and the "foetus of monarchy." To many Americans, the execuctive branch seemed as distant and threatening as the British monarchy during the recent colonial era. They feared the centralization of executive power and the nationalization of politics as much as, in our own time, people fear the globalization of the economy. A look at American geography may help explain such apprehensions.

The very physical features of the country made it difficult for Americans to think nationally. During the Adams administration, the United States had, according to the census of 1800, 5,308,483 persons (one-fifth of whom were black slaves), about a third the number of people in the British Isles and a fifth of those of the French republic. But while the people in other more established countries enjoyed a sense of national identity based on family history, a common language, and a relatively advanced system of transportation and communication, America consisted of waves of new arrivals—English, French, Irish, Germans, Dutch, Scots, all coping with a landscape for the most part undeveloped and untamed. The country had only three wagon roads, one crossing the Allegheny Mountains in Pennsylvania, another by the side of the Potomac River, and a third passing through Virginia and the Carolinas. The roads were at best a clearance through brush and forest, and travel slow, tedious, exhausting. To travel from Philadelphia, the capital, to Nashville took more than three weeks. And when Adams traveled from the capital to Quincy, which he did frequently, it took him close to a week. New England remained as distant from Virginia as the two regions had been in the early colonial era. A stagecoach left New York for Philadelphia several times a week, a trek of close to three days. Newspapers complained about the deplorable state of transportation, and it was estimated that in the northeastern states the average coach speed was four miles an hour.

Traveling on stagecoach itself was an arduous ordeal. Twelve persons poured into one wagon, cramped together with their luggage, bouncing along on rough roads, worried about floods in the spring and frozen rivers in the winter, protected from heat and cold only by leather flaps tied to the roof and sides. Travel in the North had to deal with mountains and mud slides; in the South with rivers and floods. "Of eight rivers between here and Washington," Jefferson wrote of traveling from his home in Monticello, "five have neither bridges nor boats."

Water travel could be more comfortable, but few vessels were built, and most American rivers did not flow into one another. The revolutionary hero Tom Paine drew designs for bridges, and Adams and Hamilton looked to canals as part of America's commercial development, but there was little public support for such projects. At best, Americans boarded crude flatboats and depended more on tides than on technology. In 1796, an angry Philadelphian reported a journey from New York:

> At Bordertown we went into a second boat where we met with a very sorrowful accommodation. This was about four o'clock in the afternoon. We had about twenty miles down the Delaware to reach Philadelphia. The captain, who had a most provoking tongue, was a boy of about eighteen years of age. He and a few companions dispatched a dozen or eighteen bottles of porter. We ran three different times against other vessels that were coming upstream. The women and children lay all night on the bare boards of the cabin floor. We reached Arch Street wharf about eight o'clock on the Wednesday morning, having been about sixteen hours on a voyage of twenty miles.

The difficulties and perils of travel kept Americans isolated from one another, with no national newspaper and a postal system as slow as a wagon train or flatboat. It took more than twenty days to send a letter from Maine to Georgia, and beyond the Alleghenies, any communication with the rest of the country was almost a miracle. The people of each region had their own identity and their states lived a life apart. Most politicians thought of themselves as representing their states, not the nation. An exception was Alexander Hamilton, who was born outside of America, in the Caribbean. Adams did think of the republic as a whole and saw his duty to the country at large, but he recognized that he was more welcome in Boston than in Baltimore.

Although the years 1797 to 1801 marked the presidency of John

Adams, it was essentially a Jeffersonian environment he had to contend with in his brief term in office. The country was not only
invertebrate in its incapacity to stand up as a whole, it was also inert
in its unwillingness to take on anything new and daring. Today, in
our time, America leads the world in technological development. In
the 1790s, western Europe led the world, and America felt little
need to catch up or even follow.

America was an undeveloped, agricultural society, well-off only
because of the abundance of land, but primitive, crude, and even
poor in its lack of comfort and healthy living conditions. Only in
the South did the few, rich plantation owners live well, although
the Duc de Liancourt, traveling through Virginia, reported that the
owners paid more attention to keeping up their stables than their
mansions. In New England, houses were small, thin, wooden-built
shelters, ill suited to climate, with hazardous drinking water, and
hence the population was prone to epidemics of consumption,
typhoid, scarlet fever, and diphtheria. Parts of New York City were
feeling the first flush of finance and commerce, but most of the
people still fed and clothed themselves by their household activities, and whatever was produced—homemade linens, cheese, shoes,
whale oil—was shipped abroad. Although New York started to lay
wooden pipes for supplying water, sanitary regulations went unen-
forced, and in 1798 yellow fever swept the city. European travelers
to the New World were appalled to find Americans living in such
drab, depressing conditions. Particularly revolting were their eating
habits. Salt meat at every meal, washed down with water spiked
with liquor. "I will venture to say," declared a Frenchman, "that if a
prize were proposed for the scheme of a regimen most calculated
to injure the stomach, the teeth, and the health in general, no better
could be invented than that of Americans."

John Adams watched his eating habits, but even he suffered
from colds, flus, gallstones, and gout. Health was always on his
mind. He would thank the medical doctor Benjamin Rush for sending him drugs, even a tranquilizer, as benefits bestowed from "the
love of science." But in America, science itself, despite the valiant
efforts of Ben Franklin, lagged far behind Europe.

There were several engineers in America with inventive genius.

Oliver Evans devised a locomotive steam engine, and Robert Fulton would later manufacture one. But Fulton recorded in his diary that his proposal was met with resistance and even ridicule.

More tragic was the life of John Fitch, a mechanic without education or wealth who devised a steam engine and paddles mounted onto a ferry boat. The boat performed so successfully that Philadelphians watched all summer long as it made its way against the current. Yet, while Fitch's boat succeeded, his company failed. He could raise no more money, and the public refused to use his boat or help with financing. The public, writes Henry Adams, "did not want it, would not believe in it, and broke his heart by their contempt. Fitch struggled against failure, and invented another boat moved by a screw. The Eastern public still proving indifferent, he wandered to Kentucky, to try his fortune on the Western waters. Disappointed there, as in Philadelphia and New York, he made a deliberate attempt to end his life by drink; but the process proving too slow, he saved twelve opium pills from the physician's prescription, and was found one morning dead."

In Adams's era of government, America did not lack technological genius, but the public was reluctant to support such activities, and even a navy could be thought of only because of worries about the French menace. Franklin's experiments with static electricity took place as early as 1741, but by the end of the century electrical engineering remained where it had been when he devised the lightning rod. Jefferson encouraged Franklin and David Rittenhouse, another Philadelphia scientist, to continue with their experiments to the benefit of society, but he also urged them to cease squandering their time in public service. "No body can conceive that nature ever intended to throw away a Newton upon the occupations of a crown. . . . Are those powers then, which being intended for the erudition of the world, like air and light, the world's common property, to be taken from their proper pursuit to do the commonplace drudgery of governing a single state, a work which may be executed by men of an ordinary stature, such as are always and everwhere to be found?" Science is for the exceptional, government the ordinary.

What might have been developed at the end of the eighteenth century—roads, turnpikes, public ferries, a network of canals, steam-fueled propellors, possibly the beginnings of hydroelectric power—went unexplored, and such projects did not show up on the landscape until thirty years later and the rise of the Whig Party, heir to the Federalists. In Adams's era, such developments were often associated with the Old World, where people had to pay taxes to support not only the upkeep of roads but ministers and their churches and the Crown and its luxuries. Having fled the Old World and its burdens, Americans regarded liberty as the "pursuit of happiness," which could often mean enjoying a life free of restraint and even of responsibility. Hence, we confront a paradox: a Jeffersonian America that bequeathed to the country the blessings of unalienable natural rights, and indeed bestowed the very identity of liberalism itself, turned out to be a conservative apology for the status quo. Scientists were trying to drag America into the future, but as Henry Adams observed:

> Possibly Fulton and Fitch, like other inventors, may have exaggerated the public apathy and contempt; but whatever was the precise force of the innovating spirit, conservatism possessed the world by right. Experience forced on men's minds the conviction that what had been must ever be. At the close of the eighteenth century nothing had occurred which warranted the belief that even the material difficulties of America could be removed. Radicals as extreme as Thomas Jefferson and Albert Gallatin were contented with avowing no higher aim than that America should reproduce the simpler forms of European republican society without European vices; and even this their opponents thought visionary. The United States had thus far made a single great step in advance of the Old World—they had agreed to try the experiment of embracing half a continent in one republican system; but so little were they disposed to feel confidence in their success, that Jefferson himself did not look on this American idea as vital; he would not stake the future on so new an invention. "Whether we remain in one confederacy," he wrote in 1804, "or form into Atlantic and Mississippi confederations, I believe not very important to the happiness of either part."

Jefferson's opposition to Adams and the Federalists reflected the popular inertia in a democratic society to whatever was new and innovative, whether banks, steam engines, or even taxes for national defense. Ironically, a century later, when science did take off in America along with the philosophy of pragmatism, the term *experience* meant not what had gone before but what must be faced and experimented upon in the present and future. In later industrial America, people delighted in change and transformation. In the Jeffersonian America of the late eighteenth century, however, *experience* meant just the opposite—not what should be looked into and tried but the conviction that what had been must always be. We tend to associate liberalism with political reform and social change. In Adams's era, the opposition growing around the Republicans and espousing the sentiments of Thomas Jefferson represented not reform and change but resistance to both for the purpose of restoration. One might well be curious about air and light, Jefferson told scientists, but in politics, curiosity was as dangerous as the delusion of novelty; for any step away from simplicity ran the risk of returning to monarchy and the old tyranny of taxation without representation. Hence, a rebellion could even be in opposition to the new, a reactionary rebellion springing from the tenacity of rural life. Only in America.

THE FRIES'S REBELLION

Taxmenchen, Sie Kommen! Taxmen, they are coming! In the summer and fall of 1798, the Adams administration received reports of antigovernment grumblings heard in southeastern Pennsylvania by farmers speaking German or broken English. By winter, the protests turned into actual rebellion against the federal government's tax program. Taxes, a subject that keeps accountants persevering and politicians postponing, holds up the mirror of truth to any political culture. Philosophers of the ancient republics saw fiscal impositions as necessary. "Taxes are the sinews of the state," lectured Cicero. But throughout American history, an antitax animus runs so emotionally strong that one recent president told his supporters that they had only to "read my lips" and they would never again have to worry. John Adams, in contrast, could never bring himself to mislead the people, and he knew that resorting to the imposition of taxes would please Jefferson, who delighted in seeing the administration further discredited. But such fiscal measures were necessary as America found itself in the Quasi War and the impression grew that soon the country would be in a real war and in need of arms and ships. Thus, in summer 1798, the Adams administration and the Fifth Congress introduced for the first time a system of taxation known as the Direct Tax.

The economy of the United States was in good shape when Adams took office. From revenues derived from shipping tonnage and excise taxes on items like liquor and salt, the economy had ended annually with either a balanced budget or a surplus. But the tensions due to foreign relations—the XYZ affair, the undeclared naval war with France, and the Federalist suspicion that the Directory was exporting to America the message of revolution—led Congress and the administration to increase military expenditures. During the latter two years of the administration, a Federalist Congress raised taxes to $10.5 million, almost twice the amount for normal expenditures at the beginning of the administration, and some of the increases involved the government paying off interest on loans from the Bank of the United States. Some specifics of the new taxation program bore an eerie resemblance to the Stamp Act that had precipitated the American Revolution two decades earlier. Once again there were taxes on legal documents used in business transactions, on grants, deeds, wills, and naturalization certificates. But the most controversial was the House Tax involving private residences, the first effort of the federal government to lay a direct levy on the people themselves, a method that in the past had been carried out only by state or local governments.

Aside from the quixotic policy of assessing the value of property based on how many windows a given house featured and how large they measured, the tax program developed by Hamilton and the Treasury secretary Oliver Wolcott, and approved by Adams, made every effort to be fair in distributing the burden. Houses and lands valued at less than $500 were assessed only 20 cents per hundred dollars, or 0.2 percent, whereas those over $500 paid five times the amount per hundred dollars on a graduated scale, or 1 percent. The tax on "Lands and Dwellings" to finance the Quasi War was progressive, based solely on the extent of wealth of the owner and, hence, the ability to pay.

Residents of Bucks County, and other parts of eastern Pennsylvania, saw things differently. They recalled the taxes levied years earlier that led to the Whiskey Rebellion, which seemed grossly unfair since it hit hard the single distilling economy of parts of the state. They also associated taxes with Hamilton's early effort to fund the war debts from the American Revolution, which benefited those who had bought cheap American bonds and gambled on their increased valuation. Equally suspicious, the property tax became associated with banks that dealt leniently with loans to land speculators while going so far as to foreclose the property of ordinary taxpayers. Many Pennsylvanians would revise Cicero: Taxes are the steal of the state.

In January 1799, residents in eastern Pennsylvania began to interfere with federal tax assessors, accosting them on the roads, harassing them with insults, occasionally dousing them with hot water. Resisters then held town meetings and drew up resolutions petitioning Congress for a repeal of the tax laws. Two months later the administration dispatched federal marshals who arrested resisters for obstructing the tax assessment. On March 7, as government agents were preparing to move their prisoners to a Philadelphia federal court, militiamen from Bucks County and surrounding neighborhoods converged upon the Sun Tavern in Bethlehem where the prisoners were held. The militia unit was headed by John Fries, an aging revolutionary war veteran who had at his command 150 troops, most of them also veterans, some on horse, half carrying arms. Fries, an auctioneer who had seen many property foreclosures, asserted the Sixth Amendment right that would allow his neighbors to stand trial in the "district wherein the crime shall have been committed," and he offered to make bail so that the dozen prisoners could be tried in their own courts by their own people. After a short, dramatic standoff, the chief federal marshal released the prisoners, and the crowd outside the tavern dispersed without threats or violence. But the marshal reported that the prisoners had been seized by an unruly, rebellious mob. Fries himself quietly returned to his job as a vendue crier, and he was in the midst of holding a public auction when authorities apprehended him days later.

The Fries's Rebellion is one of those minor incidents in history that became, both by historians of our time and by Adams's antagonists years before, blown all out of proportion, so much so that it contributed to Adams's loss of reelection to the presidency in 1800. Ironically, some contemporary historians, especially those who exude the radical ethos of the 1960s, find themselves in agreement with strident arch-Federalists, who expressed the conservative ethos of the 1790s. Both insist that what happened in Pennsylvania was truly radical and had the makings, had it not been repressed, of seeing the American landscape turn revolutionary. Fries and his followers represented, we are told, "the world turned upside down," a revolution from "the bottom up," a blow for freedom similar to the "slave uprising" in Virginia led by Gabriel Prosser in 1800. Where radical social historians and the arch-Federalists disagree is that the former regard the grievances of the Pennsylvanians as real and legitimate and the latter as spurious and verging on paranoia. They agree in viewing the Fries affair as the beginning of an antigovernment "movement" that posed a direct threat to social order and the authority of the republic. Even Adams, who generally kept his cool during the affair, later lost it when he told Jefferson that the Virginian knew nothing of political extremism because Virginia never had a Shays's Rebellion or a Whiskey Rebellion and "you certainly never realized the Terrorism of Fries."

In American history, a "tax revolt," whether it took place in Pennsylvania in the 1790s or in California in the 1970s, should be seen for what it was; not a radical rebellion to transform the social order but a conservative resistance to requests for payments for government services, whether needed or not. The French historian Le Roy Ladurie, unlike some American historians, has the good sense to see that a rebellion against taxes and against government can be traced from sixteenth-century France up to California's Proposition 13, and what is going on is the desire to wreak revenge upon the class that rarely had to pay taxes, the aristocracy. Hence, the French cited the classics and Roman statesmen "in every era of the Republic and the Empire who subjected the aristocrats to taxes. They taxed wealth and land in general, without considering the rank of the rich person or landowner." The French similarly cited other sources: "Cato taxing jewels, Sylla selling temple riches; Roman senators delivering their taxes in the form of copper coins heaped in a chariot."

No wonder Jacob Eyerman, a minister and supporter of Fries, warned the congregation that if they allowed the new tax policy to be implemented, the people of Pennsylvania "would be as bad off as they were in Europe." Taxes were associated with the Old World, with monarchy and the privileges of an aristocracy, the class that was often not subjected to them. But America had no aristocracy, and Adams's attempt to deliver a fair and equitable tax policy faced a mentality that assumed it had one, and that class lived high and mighty among Federalists like Hamilton and Pickering, both of whom regarded Fries as a class enemy who must be eliminated. If an aristocracy did not exist, the ordinary citizen would invent one to rationalize escaping the taxes that had historically burdened the European working poor. And the arch-Federalists, seeing ordinary tax evasion as the first step toward a jacquerie, tried to advise Adams as though America were on the verge of class warfare. The advisor Adams needed, in truth, was Alexis de Tocqueville, who would later teach America that what the country faced was not an environment of conflict but of consensus; a culture where property was safe and not threatened by the democratic masses; where a tax revolt signified the sanctity of property, not its fragility.

TO PUNISH OR TO PARDON

Much of Pennsylvania had been a Federalist stronghold until the Fries affair brought massive disaffections. Fries's sympathizers sported the tricolored cockade, danced around "liberty poles" in defiance of authorities, denounced the Federalists as "Tory snobs," and declared their loyalty to Jefferson and the Republicans. Jefferson himself remained cool to the Fries episode, and cooler still to the slave uprising led by Gabriel Prosser a year later in Virginia. To identify with what appeared to be revolution in Pennsylvania and in Virginia would be to carry on an identity with the French Revolution, about which Jefferson began to have second thoughts toward the end of the century.

Yet 1799, the time of the Fries espisode, was a tumultous year throughout the Western world. Great Britain, the once stalwart antirevolutionary country, seemed about to be on the verge of collapsing, with the Bank of England running out of cash, rebellion stirring in Ireland, and the British navy experiencing mutinies at Spithead, Nore, and elsewhere on the high seas. The Caribbean was in turmoil, with the French, English, Spanish, and Dutch all vying for control of the sugar islands, and American merchant vessels trying to escape French corsairs. In many ways the Quasi War was like our much later cold war, a time when the American people felt insecure and could scarcely tell who the enemy really was and whether the threat to the country came from without or within. Was the good, old man John Fries, so civil as to invite federal tax assessors to his house for dinner, actually a danger to the country?

Many arch-Federalists had no doubt he was, and Cobbett's *Porcupine Gazette* advocated calling out a "Provisional Army" to prepare for "civil war." Hamilton, Pickering, Fisher Ames, and others saw conspiracy in Pennsylvania, particularly when they had learned that some of the tax resisters believed that President Adams had betrothed his son John Quincy "to marry a daughter of the King of Great Britain," that "General Washington was to hold the United States in Trust for the King! And it is for these purposes," they concluded, "that an army is to be raised and *window* taxes levied." The work of French propaganda? Perhaps not. But Republican partisans told the people that the Federalist tax policy was going to confiscate their possessions and drive them into the European status of a landless peasant class.

For the Federalists, the whole issue was legal, not social. The Federalists had been raising an army not to set the stage for John Quincy Adams to put on a crown but simply to put down what appeared to be a rebellion. In March 1799, President Adams activated the Eventual Army Act, legislation passed by Congress to allow the country to send troops against any possible French-inspired insurrection. Hamilton had advised Secretary of War McHenry that "whenever the Government appears in arms it ought to appear like a *Hercules*," prepared to overawe the enemy. The quickly organized ragtag army, appearing more like a bully, had no trouble suppressing the rebels in Pennsylvania, even though the situation scarcely called for military force. But simply restoring law and order failed to satisfy some arch-Federalists. The act of resisting taxes challenged the authority of the national government to exercise its powers, and President Adams allowed himself to be persuaded by his cabinet to issue an order to put Fries and his followers on trial for offenses "which, I am advised, amount to treason." Adams then left the capital for Quincy and allowed legal matters to be handled by the cabinet.

Beginning in April, sixty offenders were brought to Philadelphia to stand trial for treason or lesser offenses. The outcome of the government's case against John Fries would establish precedent for other rulings. The sensational trial, which could very well result in the death penalty, riveted the country and polarized it politically.

To Jeffersonian Republicans, the trial symbolized all that was wrong with a government that allegedly taxed people without their consent, imposed the will of centralized power against local communities, and used the instrumentality of a judicial body appointed rather than popularly elected. To Hamiltonian Federalists, the trial symbolized the fate of national authority and the unruly, unreasonable nature of popular democracy. The arch Federalists wanted the judges to deal severely with Fries, even to the point of seeing his execution, so convinced were they that President Washington had erred in leniency toward those who had participated in the Whiskey Rebellion. The answer to the excesses of democracy was the death penalty. "Painful as is the idea of taking the life of a man," wrote Pickering to Adams, "I feel a calm and solid satisfaction that an opportunity is now presented in executing the just sentence of the law, to crush the spirit, which if not overthrown and destroyed, may proceed in its career and overthrow the government."

Prosecutors operated from the conviction, expressed in Cobbett's *Porcupine Gazette*, that "the principle of insurrection must be eradicated, or anarchy will ensue," and they argued that Fries had obstructed law in "so treasonable a manner." The two defense lawyers, Alexander Dallas and William Lewis, denied that Fries and his followers intended to "levy war against the United States," noting that once the prisoners were rescued the militia willingly disbanded. The first trial took eight days of testimony and ended in a verdict of guilty, but a juror boasting that he had accepted selection to sit in judgment on the case with his mind made up led to a mistrial. In the second trial, the presiding judge was Samuel Chase, a staunch Federalist so determined to see Fries found guilty again that he treated the jury and counsel with condescension. Politically the outcome was foreordained. Fries was sentenced to be hanged on May 23, 1800.

President Adams had no qualms about capital punishment, but Fries's conduct seemed less horrendously culpable to him than it did to the prosecution. He addressed fourteen questions to his cabinet officers to see if the meaning of treason applied to what had happened at Sun Tavern in Bethlehem the past year. The cabinet secretaries were unaminous that Fries and two others were guilty as charged of treason and that the death penalty should be carried out. But Adams, ever the independent mind, concluded that Fries and his cohorts had engaged in a rebellion, not an insurrection. "Is there not great danger in establishing such a construction of treason as may be applied to every sudden, ignorant, inconsiderable heat among a part of the people wrought up by political dispute?" he asked. The president pardoned Fries and the two cohorts convicted for treason, and the scores of others sentenced for lesser crimes. He would "take on myself alone the responsibility of one more appeal to the humane and generous natures of the American people."

The people of Pennsylvania welcomed the pardon, but the damage had been done. The sending in of troops and the prosecution itself condemned the Federalists in the eyes of the residents of Bucks County and elsewhere. The Republicans had already won over many of the Irish in America because of their mutual distrust of England; now they had the Germans in their camp as well. The president's pardon was an act of courage, a precious quality in an American politician, and one rarely rewarded in the less than "humane and generous" terrain of American electoral politics.

In the American landscape of the late 1790s, a normally hard-working, stolid, decent people rose up in protest against taxes, a display of behavior, it turns out, as American as apple pie and hot fudge sundaes. But the politics of the era misunderstood culture, dramatizing differences instead of acknowledging similarities, the common values Americans shared. Republicans hailed the Fries Rebellion as a glorious strike for liberty; Federalists denounced it as a despicable surrender to anarchy. Both factions felt threatened by the other; few considered what they had in common. John Fries, regarded as a treasonous subversive out to overturn the political culture, was really a predecessor of Ronald Reagan, the president who, in the 1980s, would tell the American people that taxes and government go hand in hand and that neither could ever be a solution to our problems since both are the problem. Significantly, Reagan's hero in American history was Thomas Paine, the same antigovernment revolutionary hero of many of our contemporary academic radicals. John Adams, alas, spent his political life trying to educate Americans to understand the value and legitimacy of government. He pardoned Fries, and his own party denounced the act as unpardonable.

8

War and Peace

ADAMS AT HOME: CHARM AND TRAGEDY

When Congress ended its session in early summer 1798, John and Abigail made a dash to Quincy. Philadelphia was succumbing to an outbreak of yellow fever that would reach an epidemic by midsummer and leave the city in a panic. The president and his wife sought to travel inconspicuously, but they were met at every town along the coach route by enthusiastic crowds. Attendance at dinners and addresses took a toll, and by the time they arrived at Quincy Abigail was ill, feverish, and completely exhausted. Doctors were summoned, the house fell into silence, and the president forsook affairs of state to stay by her bedside. "Mrs. Adams is extremely low and in great danger," he told Pickering. Their daughter Nabby, who came to help out, wrote to her brother John Quincy: "The illness of our dear mother has cast a gloom over the face of everything here, and it scarce seems like home without her enlivening cheerfulness."

In November, Adams returned to Philadelphia, bringing the gloom with him. Abigail had improved but not enough to make the trip back to the capital. Adams missed the three women in his life: Abigail, Nabby, and now the little granddaughter, "the sprightly charming Caroline," who had been the apple of his eye at Quincy.

But not all of Adams's family made for delight. There was the son Charles, a bright Harvard graduate who had been squandering money and drinking heavily, neglecting his law practice and being harassed by creditors. Charles felt dwarfed by the eminence of his father and the achievements of his two brothers, the young statesman John Quincy and the up-and-coming diplomat Thomas Boylston. On a visit to New York, the president could not get through to Charles, who would disappear on binges, abandoning his wife and two children. And when his daughter-in-law Sally gave Adams a full recital of her husband's sins, Adams poured out his soul to Abigail. "I pitied her, I grieved, I mourned," he wrote. "I renounce him," he said of his son Charles. "King David's Absalom had some ambition and some enterprise. Mine is a mere rake, buck, blood, and beast." Charles, who had once sought more than anything to emulate his father's intellectual ambitions, who had delighted the household with his gay wit and flute playing, had wasted away while his parents watched helplessly. The president left New York without having contacted his son, returning to government with a heart "loaded with sorrow."

Because of the yellow fever epidemic, the seat of government had been moved from Philadelphia to Trenton, New Jersey. Adams arrived in the city with another one of his "great colds," and, having to seek a place to stay, he settled into a simple boardinghouse with a small sitting room and bedroom. The president of the United States became, to the delight of the two maiden proprietesses, a lodger. The two women looked after Adams's ailments, to the distress of Abigail, who thought she knew better how to minister to her husband's colds as well as his spirits.

For close to a half year, Abigail was in no condition to join her husband, and he himself spent almost as much time at home in Quincy as in the executive office. While keeping an eye on Abigail's sickroom, Adams responded to a load of materials arriving by mail: requests for appointments and pardons, reports from department heads, documents requiring his signature, and, inevitably, communications about political matters among the Federalists and their factions.

Abigail remained confined to a sickbed for three months. The thought of sickness and death hovered in the atmosphere throughout the northern states. Yellow fever had hit hard the major cities of Boston, New York, Baltimore, and especially Philadelphia, where forty thousand people had been evacuated and three thousand lost their lives before the plague eased up. With his wife incapacitated,

Adams occasionally stepped forward to provide fatherly advice, though with as much wit as wisdom. He wrote to his son Thomas cautioning him about marriage and teaching the implications of the French Revolution for the future of the institution. "The source of revolution, democracy, Jacobinism . . . has been a systematical dissolution of true family authority. There can never be any regular government of a nation without a marked subordination of mothers and children to the father." But, Adams hastened to tell his son, keep this advice a secret "between you and me." If Abigail ever heard such a thought, a heresy to the heroines of the world, it would "infallibly raise a rebellion." Then Adams turned to the subject of marriage and told his son that he too had once been young "and know how tender 'tis to love. I have never dictated to my children," other than to wish them to be prudent "and not be led away by a very wild but a very fickle and transient passion."

In October John and Abigail had celebrated their thirty-fifth wedding anniversary, and, during the following month, she was well enough to travel with Nabby and Caroline to rejoin her husband in Philadelphia. Later Adams would have reservations about Abigail accompanying him to the capital's new location on a marshy mud-flat by the Potomac, which would come to be called Washington, the District of Columbia. The distance was much farther from Quincy and the living conditions primitive beyond belief, with no paved streets and the president's mansion, later to be the White House, yet to be completed and looking no more than a frame standing alone in the wilderness. The rawness and isolation of the new capital made Adams long more than ever for Quincy.

A short time earlier, on the way to Philadelphia, Abigail stopped in New York to pay a visit to Sally Adams, the forsaken wife of Charles. She was surprised to discover that Charles had returned home, but he was utterly dissipated and so ashamed and humiliated that he broke down in a sob of tears. Abigail was heartbroken to see her once handsome and joyous son reduced to misery and despair, at times shaking, rambling on and on in a slur of incoherence. Worse was to come when, on the evening that Adams heard the result of the presidential race of 1800, he also heard "of the melancholy death of a once-beloved son." John and Abigail endured the grief with faith and fortitude. "There is nothing more to be said," Adams wrote in his diary, "but let the Eternal will be done."

AMERICA AND THE "BLACK JACOBIN"

In the last two years of the Adams administration, the country had survived yellow fever only to feel the jitters of war fever. Hamilton and many arch-Federalists wanted a war with France, not only to counter the threat of revolutionary ideas in America but also as a means of expanding into territories in the west and south held by France and Spain. Congress had legislated taxes and established an army to be led by Washington, with Hamilton second in command. Some Republicans feared that an army under the Federalists could be used politically against them, a fear that grew after Washington's death in December 1799. Hamilton had considerable influence over Adams's cabinet secretaries McHenry and Pickering, and they all agreed that the president had little capacity for preparing the country for war and leading it to victory. Perhaps so. But Adams preferred the navy to the army, and at sea, the prowess of American warships improved with every battle.

At the beginning of the Adams administration, American merchant ships had suffered great losses to French privateers and other vessels operating in the Caribbean. But the resourceful secretary of navy, Benjamin Stoddard, supervised the construction and improvement of American frigates and he started a policy of recruiting seamen from schools and colleges. In February 1799, off the coast of Nevis, the *Constellation* encountered *L'insurgent*, reported to be the fastest sailing warship in the French navy. Earlier *L'insurgent*, decked with thirty-four cannons, had outfought and outsailed American and British ships. But she met her match with the *Constellation*, which maneuvered to open fire with broadsides, leaving the French vessel raked and helpless as American sailors boarded with sabers drawn and captured it. The *Constellation*'s crew and captain, Thomas Truxton, became instant heroes in America.

An even greater victory, politically and morally, involved the way Adams and Secretary of State Pickering handled relations with St.

Domingue. The island had long been the scene of a six-sided power struggle among the French, English, Spanish, Dutch, Americans, and the native islanders, later known as Haitians. Off its shores colorful sea battles took place between French corsairs and Spanish galleons carrying gold. Earlier, Voltaire had described France participating in the spoils of St. Domingue only by virtue of the boldness of Normandy sailors he called "buccaneers," *flibustier*, or freebooters, who preyed upon Spanish ships and settlements and kept the loot for themselves, in contrast to the corsairs, which sailed with "a letter of marque" and shared the booty with France. Before the French Revolution, St. Domingue had been a well-functioning colony, the most envied in the world, with the French in control of parts of it, and Britain and America sharing in commercial trade with an island that had been the most efficient producer of sugar, coffee, cotton, molasses, and rum in the West Indies.

Then suddenly, in 1791, a dramatic uprising of slaves occurred, sparking a bloody civil war that involved black insurgents, white colonialists, and several native tribal factions, including mulattoes, who had no use for blacks and at times aligned with rich planters to undertake a counterrevolution. The French revolutionary government, having abolished slavery, had second thoughts under the Directory and sent men and equipment to support its outpost in Guadeloupe and be prepared to retake St. Domingue. By 1796, with Adams coming to office, the British and Spanish had been fought to a standstill by Toussaint-Louverture, a former slave who became an astute military leader and something of a brilliant jungle Machiavelli in the game of international power politics. Secretary Pickering saw the advantage to the United States of Toussaint's rise to power and advised Adams accordingly. Adams persuaded Congress to lift an embargo on shipments to French islands, and Navy Secretary Stoddard ordered Capt. John Barry to sail his fleet off the shores of St. Domingue and raise the stars and stripes as a gesture of respect to General Toussaint. Pickering had to convince southern congressmen that Toussaint posed no threat to American interests and would not embark upon an invasion of Jamaica and other islands with slave populations.

But Jefferson was horrified. Why would America start trade relations with the "rebellious Negroes under Toussaint"? What next?

"Black crews and . . . missionaries" streaming "into the Southern states"? Toussaint was to Jefferson what Fries was to Hamilton. "If this combustion can be introduced among us under any veil whatsoever," Jefferson warned of America recognizing St. Domingue, "we have to fear it."

America's opening relations with St. Domingue must be credited to Pickering, with the support of Adams, who had no patience with proslavery apologetics. Although the Federalists were mainly concerned with the commercial advantages of trading with St. Domingue, and using the revolution in the arena of international power politics, the country's relations with an island in revolt was too much for Jefferson, who wanted to see revolution succeed everywhere in the heart of France and fail anywhere off the shores of America. Was Toussaint a dangerous radical?

A Marxist of our time, the learned, West Indies–born scholar C. L. R. James, has depicted Toussaint as a "black Jacobin," a revolutionary whose people "were closer to a modern proletariat than any group of workers in existence at the time." James even saw Toussaint as a precursor of Lenin and Trotsky, a leader who, had he been able to consolidate power, would have brought the message of class struggle to the Caribbean and perhaps to the entire western continent as well. But such concepts were alien to Toussaint, who was more influenced by the French Enlightenment. It may be more accurate to see Toussaint not as a revolutionary who sought to transform the world but as a rebel who sought to emancipate his people from colonial domination. Like the American George Washington, the Colombian Simón Bolívar, and the Cuban José Martí, Toussaint was a liberator.

But Jefferson thought otherwise, and when he was elected president he repudiated America's relations with St. Domingue and supported Napoleon's reinstalling slavery on the island. "Nothing would be easier than to furnish your army and fleet with everything," he reassured the French minister to the United States, "and to reduce Toussaint to starvation." Through deception, Toussaint was lured into a trap, captured, and sent to France where he perished in a prison. Jefferson informed Lafayette that the Declaration of Independence had no relevance to South America, a part of the world incapable of "establishing and conserving a free government." Adams's secretary Pickering could never forgive Jefferson, who looked upon Caribbean freedom fighters as guilty of only one thing, of having "a skin not coloured like our own," and thus "to reduce them to submission by starving them!" Pickering, now a senator from Massachusetts in 1806, chastised the president. "Save then your country, Sir, while you may, from such ignominy and thraldom."

President Adams and most of the Federalist leaders were northerners, and it is understandable that their views about slave uprisings would be different from those of Jeffersonian southerners, who had seen Afro-American acts of resistance and rebellion close to their own backyard. But America's relations with St. Domingue and Toussaint involved more than race. The episode deserves pondering because America, especially in the twentieth century, will still be mistaking a liberator for a revolutionary, still confusing an anticolonial war for self-determination with an international war for superpower domination. The abandonment of Toussaint and his cause was tragic, and one may well imagine how different the history of the West Indies might have been had liberal America not betrayed liberalism.

ENDING THE QUASI WAR

In early spring of 1799, the president sent a message to the Senate that fell like a bombshell. He nominated William Vans Murray, a diplomat at the Hague who had been keeping Adams informed of European developments with intelligent dispatches, to be the minister plenipotentiary of the United States to the French republic. Pickering was "totally thunderstruck," and other Federalists could hardly believe what they heard, having no knowledge whatsoever that Adams had the least intention of resuming negotiations with France after the scandalous XYZ affair. Shocked, indignant, revengeful, the Federalists did everything to scotch the idea, even challenging Murray's competency. Meanwhile, Adams temporized and put off sending Murray to Paris while he spent his time in Quincy.

The impression grew then, and it has been reinforced by some historians, that Adams had lost control of things and that he had inadvertently allowed his Hamilton-dominated cabinet to take over government while he was away from office for almost half a year. But the historian Stephen G. Kurtz demonstrates that Adams's delay in implementing his proposal to negotiate with France was deliberate, a strategy of biding time until America overcame the tensions of her domestic crises about sedition and the Fries's Rebellion, and until the situation in France became clearer and the strength of America's naval power proved itself. Then came the demise of the Directory and its replacement by Napoleon Bonaparte in November 1799, the bold general who shook the world with a series of swift victories from Austria to Egypt. The new French regime assured Adams that a mission would be received in Paris and not rejected, as was the case in the XYZ affair. In the fall of 1800, a three-man mission arrived in Paris and negotiated a peace settlement with France, called the Convention of 1800 because it was more in the nature of an arrangement than a formal treaty. It came after Adams had lost the fall election. Nevertheless, Adams, who regarded himself as more statesman than politician, would later describe the mission to France, together with his winning a loan from Holland during the Revolution and negotiating a peace treaty with England, as his greatest accomplishments.

The historian Forrest McDonald has a more critical view. "When the agreement ending the quasi-war was finally reached," he protests, "the United States had been removed as one of France's antagonists, had resumed the carrying of vital goods to France, and had sacrificed the valid spoliation claims of its citizens in the amount of $12 million. In exchange it received nothing except a cessation of hostilities that France had momentarily lost the capacity to sustain." These harsh sentiments reiterate the Hamiltonian point of view, which held that Murray and his mission would prove incompetent in dealing with wily French diplomats. The American government, it is true, did assume payment of the claims against the damage done by French warships. No doubt the Adams mission could have struck a better deal had it exploited the harm done to France's economy by the Quasi War and considered Napoleon's precarious situation facing an England in full command of the seas. At that moment in history, France needed peace with America more than America needed peace with France. Nevertheless, within months of the convention, Napoleon was marching through the Alps and winning the spectacular victory at Marengo, the beginning of the end of the old Holy Roman Empire. Looking back, Adams's French mission may have been controversial, but "in reality it was one of the most fortunate bits of negotiation that ever took place," observed the historian Edward Channing. At the Peace of Amiens, Napoleon "put an end for a year or two to the contest between Great Britain and France, and left the ocean open to the natives of France and Spain. Had America still been in conflict with the French republic, there is no telling what might have happened the moment the protection of the British fleet was withdrawn." With the British out of the picture, Adams's theory of a triangular balance of power would no longer be operative. But neither Adams nor anyone else could have predicted the power realities of Napoleonic Europe after 1800. Ironically, Napoleon was doing to Europe, or for Europe, what need not have been done for egalitarian America—abolishing feudalism and the ancien régime and making possible "careers open to talent." Like Thomas Jefferson, Napoleon Bonaparte saw no contradiction in making the world secure for liberty and making it safe for slavery.

Adams's own views on slavery resembled those of Abraham Lincoln. He too complained of "the turpitude, the inhumanity, the cruelty, and the infamy" of the institution, and Adams reminded a correspondent, "I have, through my whole life, held the practice of slavery in such abhorrence that I have never owned a Negro or any other slave." But like Lincoln, Adams worried that "the eventual total extirpation of slavery from the United States" must be approached with "prudence," lest the South be forced to secede and civil war occur.

With France in 1800, President Adams's desire for peace and opposition to war had little to do with slavery and more to do with morality and power politics. As one who had steeped himself in classical political philosophy, he recognized that the revered ancient tradition seemed to have left a modern republic with only two options: adhere to simplicity at the risk of remaining innocent or rise to strength at the risk of growing arrogant; either peace or war. "Former ages," he later wrote Benjamin Rush, "have never discovered any remedy against the universal gangrene of avarice in commercial countries but setting up ambition as a rival to it. Military honors have excited ambition to struggle against avarice, till military honors have degenerated into hereditary dignities."

Even as vice president under Washington, Adams resisted a military solution to political problems. In May 1794, Adams wrote Abigail of his brother, a Massachusetts legislator. "My brother will not vote for war, I hope, until it is necessary as well as just. Great is the guilt of an unnecessary war." As president, Adams could hardly subscribe to the classical conviction that war would bestow glory on a republic and sustain its capacity for civic virtue. Suspicious of Hamilton as a glory-hungry militarist, Adams doubted that war could be the answer to politics since both needed to be subjected to the same moral criterion. "I should have no fear of an honest war," he wrote Abigail, "but a knavish one would fill me with disgust and abhorrence." Thus spoke the Puritan who tempered the classical mystique of greatness with the cold shudder of guilt.

THE ELECTION OF 1800

In the election of 1800, John Adams was as vulnerable as a hitless batter at the plate with two strikes, two outs, no balls, and even some members of his own team wishing for a pinch hitter. For Adams had alienated his own party by sending a mission to France and pardoning Fries. And he had outraged the opposition party by passing the Alien and Sedition Acts and allowing a national army to come into existence with Hamilton at its head. Standing for peace and justice with an olive branch, Adams was too soft for conservative Federalists; standing for state authority and national security backed by force, he was too hard for liberal Republicans.

Some members of his own cabinet wanted to dump Adams. Treasury Secretary Wolcott spelled out to Fisher Ames the alleged handicaps: stubborn, too proud and temperamental, more interested in family than country, old and senile, head colds and tremors, gone in the teeth. Adams sensed his cabinet listened to Hamilton more than to the president, and after dismissing Secretary of State Pickering, he allowed Congress to carry out the dismantling of Hamilton's long-sought army. When George Cabot heard that Hamilton was composing an indictment against the president, he reminded the New Yorker that the Federalists had endorsed Adams and Charles Pinckney (former general and diplomat) in a party caucus in Philadelphia. Hamilton had no problem with Pinckney, but goaded by War Secretary McHenry he allowed his report to be leaked to the press, "The Public Conduct of John Adams, Esq., President of the United States."

An enraged Hamilton questioned Adams's patriotism and integrity, accused him of going against Washington's wish for a permanent army, and of humiliating the country by sending a mission to France. Hamilton thought it was his duty to let the people know that the president "does not possess the talents adapted to the *administration* of government, and that there are great and intrinsic defects in his character, which unfit him for the office of chief magistrate."

The Republicans rejoiced at the report. Adams, Hamilton, and Pinckney now stood quarrelsome before the public, fighting among themselves to the detriment of their own party. Jefferson, too covert to be controversial, seemed the only worthy candidate. But in the background remained a potential candidate more covert and devious than even Jefferson himself—Aaron Burr.

The handsome and gallant Burr had fought in the Revolution and earned the rank of colonel while finding time for womanizing and luxury. The schemer and scoundrel would later, in the era of Jefferson's presidency, become nortorious for the duel in which he shot and killed Hamilton and for standing trial for treason on the charge that he was attempting to separate western sections of the country from the republic. Earlier, his ambitions were more vertical. With a talent for politics and a lust for power, in the 1790s he became a New York assemblyman, state attorney general, and U.S. senator, and in the process used rival factions to unseat Philip Schuyler, Hamilton's father-in-law. He organized the New York City elections with such efficiency and self-promotion that he was rewarded with the Republican Party's choice for the vice presidency. Burr's role in the election of 1800 would prove to be the most telling of all candidates, but to this day few can figure out what he had in mind for America or for himself. The term associated with Aaron Burr is *enigmatic,* so inscrutable as to defy even Adams's keen sense of human motivation. "As usual, he was mysterious," writes Burr's admirer Gore Vidal. "He makes even a trip to the barber seem like a plot to overthrow the state."

The presidential contest of 1800 was strictly a count of the electoral college vote, which meant that the parties in control of the assemblies would determine the outcome in a race among states rather than people. The count continued through the month of December. In the first week Adams and Pinckney were ahead of Jefferson and Burr. Predictably, Massachusetts and New England went for Adams and Virginia and much of the South for Jefferson. But Pennsylvania and New York turned out a Republican vote. The final count gave Jefferson seventy-three, Burr seventy-three, Adams sixty-five, Pinckney sixty-three. Adams received the news of his defeat on the evening he heard of the death of his son.

The Federalist defeat of 1800 has often been blamed on the president. He did lose Pennsylvania due to his tax policy, but the Alien and Sedition Acts seemed to have little effect on the vote, since Jefferson did no better electorally in Kentucky and Virginia in 1800 than he did in 1796. In fact, Adams had more electoral votes in 1800 than in 1796. The difference was New York, where Adams lost to Burr's machinations with city voting turnout and to the New Yorker Hamilton's refusal to support his own party's candidate. Indeed, Hamilton enjoyed the role of kingmaker. With the Republican vote a tie and the selection sent to the House, where the vote remained in deadlock after numerous ballots, Hamilton, distrustful of Burr as a dangerous demagogue, persuaded a Federalist Congress to break the tie and join the Republicans in designating Thomas Jefferson as president. Jefferson, the democrat of the people, owed his election to his rival who termed the people "a great Beast!" Adams owed nothing to anyone.

Adlai Stevenson, the Democratic candidate who lost twice in running against Dwight Eisenhower in the 1950s, knew the emotion

Adams had experienced. "Someone asked me, as I came in, down on the street, how I felt, and I was reminded of a story that a fellow townsman of ours used to tell—Abraham Lincoln," Stevenson said of his Springfield, Illinois, political ancestor. "They asked him how he felt once after an unsucessful election. He said he felt like a little boy who had stubbed his toe in the dark. He said he was too old to cry but it hurt too much to laugh."

Adams too felt that life would never be the same, and he also managed to overcome malice with mirth. But for a person who scarcely cared for the wheeling and dealing of politics, he could look forward, as did Abigail, to returning to Quincy. "Be not concerned for me," he wrote to his much-concerned son Thomas. "I feel my shoulders relieved from a burden. The short remaining of my days will be the happiest of my life."

Adams's days of retirement at Quincy would be far from short. But before leaving the capital, he was busy seeing through the settlement with France, asking for the resignation of unloyal cabinet members, and having Congress pass a judiciary bill creating new judgeships to handle the increasing court load. Adams's critics called these efforts "midnight appointments," a last, desperate effort of an outgoing president to stack the judicial system with Federalist partisans. But Adams had always believed in the independency of the judicial branch of government, and with the position vacant on the Supreme Court, he appointed John Marshall as chief justice, the Virginian who had opposed the Alien and Sedition Acts.

On March 4, 1801, Adams quietly departed from the president's house and the capital in the dark hours of the early morning. At noon that day, Jefferson galloped up to the Capitol, strapped his horse to a fence, entered the Senate chamber, and took the oath of office. Adams had been criticized for not staying to attend the inauguration of his successor. He probably should have, for appearances' sake. But there was no precedent for such a ceremonial transfer of the guard, and to this day no one seems to know if Adams had even received an invitation.

"LINES OF EXHILARATION":
LIFE AND LETTERS AT QUINCY

John Adams rode in a coach five hundred miles, partly through a violent storm, to set his feet down on the solid ground of his Quincy farm, where he found in the barn a hundred-pound load of seaweed, vital fertilizer for his fields. At sixty-six, he was home for good, and there he knew he would die. Often, he thought back on his loss, feeling rejected by the American people to whom he had devoted his political life, perhaps forgetting that the people scarcely gave Jefferson a majority vote and that had it not been for Burr, he would still be in office. Adams just as often told friends and neighbors that at Quincy he was enjoying the time of his life.

The house, now so expanded to be called "Adams Mansion," bustled with friends, relatives, visitors, children, and grandchildren. Charles's widow, Sally, was there with her two children, as was Thomas's wife, Ann, and her two. Adams was delighted to be around the young, so full of energy, curious, mischievous, lively. The kids rescued him from his boredom and bouts of mild depression, and he responded to their teasing and titters more than Abigail, the maternal disciplinarian.

Adams was, as the New England saying goes, "penny poor and property rich." He had little money, and the small savings he accumulated he lost investing with the Bank of London, although the securities that Abigail had bought on her own came in handy. At his age, he did not think of resuming a law practice. But he occupied himself with his abundant land—planting, watering, distributing compost, battling bugs on the fruit trees. Working in the natural world often turned his thoughts toward the philosophical world, wondering whether a microscope expanded knowledge or limited it, whether insects were a curse or a blessing, whether a benevolent God could be reconciled with an evil world.

Did Adams, with his passion for prose and poetry, have a desire to write his autobiography? In our present time, publishers would be at the door of an ex-president with a contract for millions, and many of the memoirs would be ghosted. But in Adams's era, memoirs could be regarded as self-serving and mercenary, and even

Jefferson, as destitute as he was after he left office, would neither write nor speak for money. Adams did consider writing an autobiography to offer a narrative of his personal life and political career. But he realized how careless he had been in keeping his papers in order, and the thought of the act of recollecting proved too painful. "It is a delicate thing to write from memory," he confessed to John Quincy. "To me the undertaking would be too painful. I cannot but reflect upon the scenes I have beheld."

But if Adams abandoned prose, he could not help but to continue thinking of politics, not with his career in mind but with the nature of the beast itself. Whereas his descendant Henry Adams discerned the entropy of chaos in politics, he saw a pattern of coherence, a continuous alternation. One party, the conservatives Adams specified, would hold power for about a dozen years, and the more liberal side would then succeed for a similar period. The Jeffersonian Republicans would stay in office for around sixteen years and then inevitably there would be a response. "Our government will be a game of leapfrog of factions, leaping over one another's back about once in twelve years according to my computation." In our era, the historian Arthur Schlesinger Jr. developed a "cyclical" theory of American history somewhat along the same lines. But the Adams-Schlesinger theory leaves us with a question to be explored in the conclusion: Did the Jeffersonians really leapfrog over the Federalists? Or did they simply mate with them as they shared the same pond, living in a habitat of consensus while croaking with conflict?

Adams's thoughts on politics and philosophy did little to take his mind away from the health and condition of his family and friends. A dozen years after he left office, now in his late seventies, the country he knew seemed to be the land of the dying. Abigail's closest friends, Mary and Richard Cranch, wasted away in illness and died. Daughter Nabby had to have a breast removed only to be soon taken by cancer. Benjamin Rush died of typhus. Adams's old loyal supporter Elbridge Gerry died shortly after a few other friends passed away, leaving him depressed with the thought that "now not one of my contemporaries and colleagues is left." Son-in-law, William Smith, died with his daughter Caroline at his bedside.

John and Abigail felt lonelier than ever. Then, the last bond that held the family together broke for good with the passing of Abigail, who had suffered a sudden stroke, in October 1818, and for days could neither move nor speak. She died peacefully on November 10, surrounded by children and grandchildren. Adams was devastated. In their fifty-four years of marriage, Abigail, ten years younger, although ill at times, always seemed the robust, healthier partner. Now she was no more, and Adams hardly cared whether he lived or died. "The bitterness of death is past," he wrote; "the grim spoiler so terrible to human nature has no sting left for me."

It may well be the wisdom of a benevolent deity, Adams's friend Benjamin Rush once speculated, to arrange life so that the human faculties diminish with old age and by the time death is at the door, the dying one is too gone to feel the dread. But Rush's friend Jefferson also knew that death is a greater ordeal for the living, and he wrote Adams to express his grief and to speak of a time when they both "must ascend in essence to an ecstatic meeting with friends we have loved and lost, and whom we shall still love and never lose again. God bless and support you under your heavy affliction."

The note comforted Adams, who had been conducting a long exchange of letters with Jefferson for the past half-dozen years. Years earlier, the correspondence had been suggested by Rush, in the hope of reconciling the two statesmen he so admired and make it possible for them to put aside their differences and what he thought may be little more than misunderstandings. But Abigail had been in a correspondence with Jefferson before her husband, and for the wife there were no misunderstandings at all but simply unscrupulous, political behavior she called upon Jefferson to explain. Emphasizing that her communication would be kept secret, she demanded to know why Jefferson had stood by, instigated, and even supported attacks on her husband by Callender and other yellow journalists. Jefferson rationalized his financial aid to Callender as "no more meant as encouragements to his scurrilities than those I give to the beggar at my door," as though he had no concern how the money was used. Jefferson's denial of bankrolling the press against Adams was "disingenuous," the historians Ellis and McCullough have concluded.

But while Abigail was unforgiving, Adams himself found a certain fulfillment in his voluminous correspondence with Jefferson. The exchange of letters would conclude, as the two authors both faced death, with a burst of affection, but the epistolary relationship reads like a running argument without end, as though each writer were searching for some idea or principle upon which they could agree. Adams, who believed that differences were inevitable, would not allow Jefferson to think differently; Jefferson, who believed in the natural harmony of human nature, would not cease exchanging conflicting views. We are told that differences begin in pride and end in anger. With Adams and Jefferson, they end in love.

The correspondence seemingly covered every subject under the sun: the truth and falsity of Christianity, the promises of science, the conceit of American providence, the relevance and irrelevance of the classics, the sources of morality and virtue, the wisdom and folly of the French *philosophes*, the validity of archaeological findings, the riddle of freedom and fate, the proposition of equality and the reality of hierarchy, the distinction between a "natural" and "artificial" aristocracy, the responsibility of generations, and, a subject Jefferson said he was no longer interested in, government itself. It must have been tempting to Adams to chide Jefferson for having been wrong about so many historical developments, from the French Revolution he wanted to avow, to the War of 1812 he wanted to avoid. But for the most part Adams restrained himself, except for an occasional dig: "What think you of terrorism, Mr. Jefferson?"

Adams had also a prolific correspondence with Mercy Otis Warren and John Taylor of Caroline, both of whom had written books claiming that Adams favored an aristocratic monarchy and that he allowed his revolutionary principles to be corrupted. "Corrupted Madam!" he exploded to Warren. "What provocation, what evidence . . . Corruption is a charge I cannot and will not bear—I challenge the whole human race . . . to produce an instant of it from my cradle to this hour." No one ever responded to Adams's challenges, not even Jefferson. But the Adams-Jefferson correspondence remains one of the richest documents in American intellectual history. In their twilight years, many ex-presidents, like old warrior generals, simply fade away. The thoughts and writings of Adams and Jefferson not only do not fade but remain to radiate reflections that are as fresh today as when they were written two centuries ago.

As Adams approached ninety, he found he could barely move around or hold a pen. General Lafayette paid him a visit and hardly recognized the waning, decrepit old man who had once been a young rebel. But in late 1824, Adams perked up as he followed the race for the presidency, which had his son John Quincy facing off against Andrew Jackson. Adams admired Jackson, the hero of the Battle of New Orleans and a frontiersman suspicious of eastern bankers, the boon of Hamilton, the bane of Adams.

He was, of course, pulling for his son, who became the sixth president of the United States. Immediately, Jefferson wrote to congratulate the father who had brought up a son to be chosen as the leader of our country. Jefferson, who had no son, struck the right note. "Nights of rest to you and days of tranquility are the wishes I tender you." Adams wept with joy, and he told Jefferson to regard John Quincy Adams as "our son," an heir to all the generation of '76. "Every line from you exhilarates my spirits and gives me a glow of pleasure," he replied to Jefferson. "I look back with rapture to those golden days when Virginia and Massachusetts lived and acted together like a band of brothers and I hope it will not be long before they may say *redeunt Saturnia regna*" [the golden age is returning].

On July 1, 1826, John Adams, weak and delirious, fell into a coma. The previous day he had been asked to provide some last thoughts on the forthcoming celebration of the fiftieth anniversary of the Declaration of Independence. "I will give you," he replied, "Independence forever," that is all; the two simple words suffice. On the Fourth of July, John Adams and Thomas Jefferson, once having fought together as revolutionary friends, and then falling out as political foes, left the world as a "band of brothers."

Conclusion:
The Moralist in Politics

John Adams has often been regarded as something of a loser. An important political philosopher and a president of the United States who can be praised for his honesty and integrity, yet a loser nonetheless. The party of George Washington, having led the country in the 1790s, became Adams's party, and it was never again to win the presidency after 1800. In American history, the Federalists disappeared from the map, a species incapable of succeeding or surviving. To think of Adams, therefore, is to think of failure, perhaps a noble failure, but still one to be remembered more in sorrow than in celebration.

This negative assessment rests on three questionable impressions. First, that America really witnessed a "Revolution of 1800," as Jefferson hailed his election and the Republicans claimed it to be. Supposedly, the country had turned the corner, with one political ideology triumphing over the other in a culture of intense conflict. The second impression is that in a fair fight, Jefferson beat Adams, and the Virginian must be declared the winner even though the democrat who always claimed to represent the majority failed to win it. The third impression builds on the other two. Accordingly, in the course of American political development after 1800, it was the Jeffersonian Republicans who proved to have a better grasp of the nature of reality and of the direction of history. The waning of federalism, so the story goes, proved the wisdom of republicanism.

These three impressions—the first resting on the premise of conflicting, incompatible ideologies; the second on the premise that Jefferson fought fair and square even though he needed the Hamilton he hated to win the office he coveted; the third on the premise that the future verified the past, that what came to be was meant to be—are part of the conventional wisdom of American history. The assumptions would leave Adams down and out, dead and buried without a record or even an autospy. And without an investigation into why Adams passed away politically, we would accept his whimsical quip, in a letter to John Taylor in 1815, that the Federalists "commited suicide," having "killed themselves and the national president . . . at one shot, and then, foolishly or maliciously, indicted me for the murder." Who killed whom? To study what happened to John Adams may enable us better to appreciate his predicament and, as well, to understand American history for what it really is: a study not of leapfrog factions or of conflicting ideologies, but of emerging interest-driven, factional blocs struggling for dominance within a political culture of consensus. Politics, the organization of suspicion, has power as its object.

Rather than regarding the "Revolution of 1800" as a revolution, for example, it would be more enlightening to appreciate the difference between an election and a convulsion. The election of 1800 was, indeed, a momentous turning point in modern history, but not for the reasons usually claimed, particularly by the Republicans, who were hailing the French Revolution apparently with no idea that it represented the very centralization of power that should have filled them with dread. Instead of a revolution, the election of 1800 marked the first time that a government, deriving from a violent revolution, went on to enjoy a peaceful and orderly transfer of power. The outs had replaced the ins, and not a shot was fired nor a back stabbed; no guillotines and no knifing in the bathtub of Jean-Paul Marat by Charlotte Corday, symbolizing a liberty born of reason killed by enthusiasm. The phenomenon of a real social revolution, we should keep in mind, takes place in an environment of oppression where there is no possible means of change and liberation other than resorting to force and violence. But even with older republics subjected to civil wars, the scenario had been troubling.

When thinkers of the eighteenth century dwelled on such regimes, they were struck by their fragility and their politics of gore and the ways they were overthrown in bloody feuds. Here is Adams quoting from Machiavelli's *History of Florence* in his *Defence*:

> Greater certainly and more cruel is the resentment of the people when they have recovered their liberty, than when they are acting in defence of it; and an instance of brutal ferocity happened here that is a disgrace to human nature. The people insisted upon some persons being delivered up to them, and among a father and son; when these were brought out and delivered up to the thousands of their enemies; and though the son was not eighteen, yet neither his youth nor his innocence, nor the gracefulness of his person, were sufficient to protect him from the rage of the multitude. Many who could not get near enough to reach them whilst they were still alive, thrust their swords into them after they were dead; and not content with this, they tore their carcasses to pieces with their nails and teeth, that so all their senses may be glutted with revenge; and after they have feasted their ears with their groans, their eyes with their wounds, and their touch with tearing the flesh off their bones, as if all this was not enough, the taste likewise must have its share and be gratified.

When Adams studied the past, he sought to know what was happening in the streets. The history of republics is the history of liberty but also of brutality, cruelty, cunning, murder, even sadism. It is also the history of the transitory as well as the tragic, of finitude and death. At America's Constitutional Convention in 1787, it was emphasized that republics "flourish only to vanish," and the framers feared the thought of a political regime fated to perish. Thirteen years later, however, in 1800, the new American republic appeared to be flourishing and stabilizing at the same time, and an opposition party came to power without America shedding a single drop of blood, an achievement made possible by the procedural system that would be inherent in the Constitution that the *Federalist* authors devised and Adams defended, a Constitution established so that America need not again go through a revolution. Jefferson may have believed that the future of liberty depended upon the sovereignty of the states, but his own victory in 1800 depended on the Constitution and the House of Representatives that stood for the nation as a whole. Once in office as president, Jefferson used the political apparatus that Adams had bequeathed to America.

In more ways than one, the future of America depended upon Adams rather than Jefferson. Jefferson was serenely confident that he could identify with the democratic masses, convinced that no matter where he stood, or what he stood for, he always stood for the majority, and when he looked into the faces of the people, he saw himself. The more anguished Adams looked into the faces of the people and saw a blur and heard a cacaphony of tongues, not a coherent public but a heterogeneous multitude that no single person or institution could possibly represent, other than mediating their differences. Jefferson, in contrast, sought to see only unanimity, as he advised John Taylor in the middle of the Adams administration:

> Seeing that we have somebody to quarrel with, I had rather keep our New England associates for that purpose than to see our bickerings transferred to others. They are circumscribed within such narrow limits, and their population so full, that their numbers will ever be the minority, and they are marked, like the Jews, with such a perversity of character as to constitute, from that circumstance, the natural division of our parties. A little patience, and we shall see the reign of witches pass over, their spells dissolved, and the people recovering their true sight, restoring their government to its true principles.

Jefferson advises the Republicans to project their own quarrels onto the Federalists and look upon New Englanders as rootless Jews forever destined to be a minority. It should be pointed out that in later correspondence Adams defends the Jews against the charge of "perversity of character," patiently explaining to Jefferson, as the historian Richard Samuelson documents, the wisdom of the Hebrew religion. But the more immediate issue is that anyone in opposition to Jefferson is by definition a minority, even though the doctrine of state sovereignty he initiated, and John C. Calhoun later propounded, presumed the South was a minority fighting for its survival against the North and West. In Jefferson's era, Virginia may have been able to see itself as representing the majority since America was then a rural, agricultural society. But America developed in ways that left Jeffersonianism behind, and today the farming states represent a diminishing minority of the population, and their only power remains with the Senate, the very institution that the Virginian distrusted and the New Englander defended. Again Jefferson lives through Adams.

Such ironic twists seem to have eluded historiography. With the transition from Adams to Jefferson, the focus is on 1800, a year at once tumultuous and bitter. In the presidential race, Republicans accused Federalists of oppressing liberty and betraying the republic. The pseudo-president, the "Duke of Braintree," was planning to marry one of his sons to a daughter of George III, and thus America would awake one day to discover it had an inherited monarchy and had been reunited with England. Federalists, for their part, accused Republicans of subversion and sedition, with Jefferson depicted as an atheist and immoralist who would deliver the country to the debauchery of the French. Yale graduates were warned that if they voted for Jefferson their degrees would be revoked. In the rhetoric of accusation and mudslinging, 1800 put America through political purgatory. On Inauguration Day, with the president-elect about to be sworn in, the Federalist *Gazette* described the capital city as taken over by a throng armed with guns and sticks, "a motley group" with "a savage leader and his tribes." What were these mobs up to? "Their object was to *honor* the President," the *Gazette* mocked, "yea to honor him!!!!!!" The Jacobins had arrived!

THE ADAMS ERA AND THE NEW HISTORY

At the end of the presidency of John Adams, America was experiencing a curious paradox: the stability of political institutions in the face of fierce political emotions. Today, many of our contemporary historians, instead of emphasizing the solidity of institutions and the strength of society, concentrate their attention on the emotions and suspicions of a culture of fear and accusation. The implication is that the near-hysteria of the era was more real than contrived and that what Adams was accused of should be taken seriously since the people, or at least much of the people, believed it. This way of looking at the past derives from new orientations toward the study of history. A subject in the past, like Adams, for example, should be approached not in light of what he himself thought, felt, wrote, or did but how he came to be represented, depicted in the press and in such visual media as cartoons, and what determines how he is represented can be grasped by examining the language of the era, the words and phrases used to describe him. When historians do examine the political language of the Adams period, they see rampant discord and distrust, and the challenge is to try to explain what accounts for America having so divisive a political culture of conflict.

The divisiveness has been attributed to several sources. In 1800, America still clung to older aristocratic notions of honor, including the practice of dueling. Hence, issues of governance became less public and more personalized while reputations were open targets for insults and slanders in an era when dissent became synonymous with disloyalty. In addition to the climate of incivility, the Adams era also found itself in an international context where events abroad were more troubling than developments at home. It was, moreover, a time when old systems of authority were fading, the residual sentiments of monarchy, hierarchy, deference, and aristocracy, and with the passing of the old order no new national identity had yet emerged. Some historians go so far as to use the postmodernist idea of "the other" to demonstrate how former colonists became suspicious of anything or anyone different from themselves. Engaging in a "rhetorical othering," factions become exclusive and view one another as dangerously alien, subversive monarchists or Jacobins. In this respect, Adams's failure was his inability to establish a national identity, a unitary vision that would have made all Americans feel at one with themselves.

No doubt America lacked a "vital center" in the late 1790s, with mobs squaring off and politicians coming to blows, and in historical scholarship it has even been suggested that had Jefferson lost to Adams, there could well have been a civil war. During the election year, Republicans in several regions had organized armed militias ready to come out of the woods to do battle with Hamilton and his ever-ready army. It seemed that the *Federalist* authors were mistaken in thinking that distrust would hold the country together in a kind of equipoise of suspicion. But it was the leader of the Republicans, not the Federalist president, who accused his antagonist of disloyalty to the principles of the republic. Why blame Adams for the mental condition of America? Stymied by Hamilton, who regarded him as too unreliable to hold the office, President Adams was stalked by Jefferson, who regarded him too unfaithful to run the country.

According to the approach of the new history, we should look to language and the aggressive construction of images on the part of both the Republicans and the Federalists. The problem with interpretations based on this approach is that the deeper motives behind the suspicions and accusations go unexplored. Adams was no more a monarchist than Jefferson was a Jacobin, though both were what later came to be called "fellow travelers"—those who thought that political institutions and ideologies may be appropriate for a foreign country but had no place in America. With the exception of the work by Ellis and McCullough, much of the current interpretation of the Adams era fixates on the language of Republicanism. The struggle between the Federalists and the Republicans emerges as a replay of the "court" versus "country" factions of old England politics, with power and intrigue on one side and people and virtue on the other: "corrupt court and worthy country." The interpretation ignores what Adams had noted in his *Defence*, where he cites Thucydides instructing us that the language of politics is determined by the politics of language. When Jefferson accuses Adams of being a monarchist, and of New England Federalists as being as displaced as the "Jews," he was certainly engaging in "rhetorical othering." But to what purpose? Eighteen hundred was the first democratic election that saw two parties vying with each other, and for one to win office, or the other to hold on to it, neither could run on a platform of consensus and unanimity. Instead they had to exaggerate antagonism and diversity. Once the election is over, however, the winning side urges the nation to forget all past disputes and dedicate itself to coming together, now invoking the dictum that we are all one and the same—"All Republicans, all Federalists."

If America really witnessed the "Revolution of 1800," one might expect some murmur of a possible counterrevolution or at least hear the voice of a distinct opposition. Instead, Federalists watched Republicans become the clones of consensus. Although Adams had left the Treasury with a surplus, Jefferson did carry out his pledges to cut back expenditures and taxes, eliminate military appropriations, and do whatever he could to chip away at the power of the judiciary. But the banking system remained intact and the authority of the national government augmented, far more than under Adams, as Jefferson negotiated the Louisiana Purchase and imposed an embargo on the New England states. Without ever acknowledging it, Jefferson fulfilled Hamilton's dream of making America into an empire with a nation-state, to the despair of old pure Republicans like John Taylor of Caroline. It would not be the only time in American history when a political party succeeded by becoming that which it once opposed.

Looking back, the contests between the Republicans and Federalists became so bitter and intense not because the language of the era suggests real, profound differences but because it concealed what each party was after: power, the satisfaction of ruling and controlling, of being free of insecurity and suspicion, especially a suspicion that may tell us more about the suspicious than the suspected. Jefferson did not trust Adams because he convinced himself that the president was a monarchist, and he claimed that evidence of such a position could be found in Adams's own writings, an open book for all to read. But the accusation need not be documented when it is in the nature of politics to express suspicion rather than to establish it. In a letter of July 13, 1813, Adams directly challenged Jefferson to prove his accusation:

In truth, my "Defence of the Constitutions" and "Discourses On Davila," were the cause of immense unpopularity which fell like the tower of Siloam upon me. Your steady defence of democratical principles, and your invariable favorable opinion of the French revolution, laid the foundation of your unbounded popularity. *Sic transit gloria mundi.*

Now, I will forfeit my life, if you can find one sentiment in "Defence of the Constitutions," or the "Discourses on Davila," which, by a fair construction, can favor the introduction of monarchy or aristocracy to America. They were all written to support and strengthen the Constitution of the United States.

Jefferson declined the challenge. Why not? The damage had been done. In truth, Adams was trying to strengthen the Constitution by offering America not the dogma of absolute monarchism but the doctrine of political institutionalism, the "machinery of government" and all its checks and controls. But if any stigma can beat a dogma, the fate of Adams proves that any distortion can beat a doctrine.

John Adams has often been called the "philosopher of authority" and Thomas Jefferson the "apostle of liberty." Such terms obscure what was really going on in the election of 1800. Not only did Jefferson exercise far more authority when he became president but his own passion for liberty rendered him suspicious of power anywhere beyond his own capacity to wield it. "Men desire to be in control," observed Bertrand Russell, "because they are afraid that the control of others will be used unjustly to their detriment." For those who seek to dominate, their "love of power" goes unmentioned as it represents "an embodiment of fear." Jefferson feared the "apostate" president who had lost his soul to "the harlot of England," and time and again he warned the country about the "monarchization" of the republic and of Adams having been blinded by the "glare of royalty," even hinting that Adams's refusal to support the French Revolution reflected a weak commitment to the American Revolution on the part of a closet counterrevolutionist. At the same time Hamilton knew Adams was no monarchist; he was worse! A nonaggressive president whose weaknesses threatened to sink the government, Adams was more interested in peace than war and more inclined to pardon rebels than to punish them. In American history, the familiar politics of fear, suspicion, and accusation begin as far back as Virginia in the 1790s, when opposition politics had no rules of discourse and its rhetoric no basis in reality. Looking back, American history felt the first stirrings of Joseph McCarthy in the machinations at Monticello, and Hamilton emerges as the fifth columnist of the Federalists, a party leader who preferred the Republican opposition to his own president remaining in power.

WHY JEFFERSON COULD NOT ANSWER ADAMS'S QUESTIONS

The perspectives of Adams and Jefferson require scrutiny. Except for Lincoln, Madison, and John Quincy Adams, and possibly Woodrow Wilson and Theodore Roosevelt, Adams and Jefferson were the first and the last of the "thinking" presidents, the rare few who try to leave America with a better understanding of itself and its relation to the world. Although the rich correspondence between Adams and Jefferson concludes in a burst of brotherly affection, as each was approaching death, the bulk of it is, like their lives, a long argument without end. Their differences remained unyielding, and Americans were asked then, as we are still asked now, two basic questions: Are we to trust people or institutions? Does the meaning of America lay in consensus or conflict?

Did America really need all of Adams's mechanistic checks and controls? Jefferson, to his credit, did see what Adams failed to consider: The Constitution was not necessary to control democracy since the people themselves posed no serious threat to liberty and property. The idea of a "mixed government" could not possibly work if America really had social classes poised against one another, as Alexis de Tocqueville would later point out. Indeed, the Constitution that Adams envisioned, where the Senate was to represent the wealthy few and the House the struggling many, scarcely developed that way in a country that would have no clear-cut class divisions. Adams's hope for the "independence" of the executive branch seems unrealistic in view of his own worry that American politics would be infected with the "gangrene of greed."

The great fear of both Adams and Jefferson was fear of corruption, with one thinker seeing it emanating from money and avarice, the other from monarchy and aristocracy. For Jefferson, the people themselves could rarely be the source of the problem, and thus he tells Adams that the ancient Roman republic was "steeped in corruption vice and venality" due to the "degenerate Senate," making impossible a return to true virtue and liberty. To Adams, once a regime starts to face the future and begins to develop and modernize, there is little chance for the restoration of civic virtue and the classical return to first principles. "Will you tell me how to prevent riches from becoming the effects of temperance and industry?" Adams asked Jefferson as late as 1819. "Will you tell me how to prevent riches from producing luxury? Will you tell me how to prevent luxury from producing effeminacy intoxication extravagance Vice and folly?"

Jefferson had no answer because his eyes were fixed on the institutions of the Old World at a time when America was moving ahead and leaving history and its antiquated institutions behind. Jefferson's hopes may have had to do with the future, but his fears were rooted in the past. Adams, in contrast, feared for the future, precisely where we are today, knowing well that the democratic masses will "emulate" the upper orders as riches and the culture of consumption overtake the republic. In conventional narratives of American history, Jefferson's victory over Adams is regarded as the story of the forward momentum of freedom, the triumph of democracy over aristocracy. But Adams doubted that human character changes as political regimes change, and his insights about economic behavior anticipate postmodernist thinkers in warning us that democracy emboldens envy and puts money on the throne.

Jefferson also had no answer to Adams's questions because he himself loved luxury and, as a voracious consumer indebted to his creditors, hated banks. The French, noting how he eagerly had his country purchase the Louisiana Territory and then had his eyes on Canada, regarded the American president as an acquisitive aristocrat on the make. Jefferson, Paine, and other Republicans championed the French Revolution as the death of monarchy and had no qualms about the new life of money. As Edmund Burke pointed out, the revolution's confiscation of the lands of gentry and Church turned France "into one great game table" where opportunity was open for all to speculate and gamble, releasing the "impulses, passions, and superstitions of those who live on chances." Today many Americans partake of the same temptation, investing in the stock market and then screaming bloody murder when they lose their shirt. What good is liberty without prosperity? The bankruptcy of monarchy freed up money to the delight of democracy, and while Jefferson was buying his prestigious paintings on credit, Adams was trying to save his few pennies.

But John Adams couldn't win no matter how many times he tried to explain his view of the world. Because *Discourses on Davila* dared to deal with the desire for wealth, Adams's critics accused him of being an aristocrat defending riches, when he was actually a moralist admonishing it. Far from a sign of salvation, excessive wealth was a sign of sin, as original as it was inevitable.

But here one runs up against a serious limitation on Adams's part when it comes to understanding the American character. Adams saw little relationship of wealth to work, what later came to be known as the "Protestant ethic." As a result, he failed to see that beneath all his structures of political controls designed to balance power there would be a widespread moral sentiment that respected property and rendered it safe from democracy. Both the *Federalist* authors and Adams believed that the Constitution was necessary to control conflict; but what actually made the system work was consensus, the values the country shared in common regarding the relation of labor to property. The American people believed in hard work and frugality and were willing to strive and sacrifice to enjoy the good things in life. Such a mentality was at the root of capitalism in early colonial America. As Max Weber noted in his famous thesis of 1905, that outlook grew out of a theology of torment over the fate of one's soul; an angst about salvation that drove the body to try to work its way to heaven; and a spiritual longing that proved unable to survive modernity, where the contemporary world experiences the delirious fever of capitalism without the disciplining faith of Christianity—Hong Kong without hell. Thus, while Adams may have insufficiently appreciated the Protestant ethic in early

American history, he clearly presaged modern thinkers who fore-saw the waning of an older morality as reason comes to be driven by power and greed. It is not what people claim to have a right to, as an aspect of natural law, which was the outlook in the eighteenth century; it is simply what they desire and seek by any means possible.

Such was the situation later faced by President Theodore Roosevelt. He realized that America would need to assert the authority of the nation-state to contend with the willpower of the "malefactors of wealth," as though he had to use Hamiltonian means to deal with Hamiltonian mutants. The one president who may have fulfilled Adams's aspirations was Theodore Roosevelt, the nationalist. He disdained Jefferson's belief that America could have a foreign policy without a navy and shared Adams's conviction about a strong executive branch. Roosevelt expressed the same scorn for a wealthy class that gives America nothing more than "effeminacy intoxication extravagance."

Yet when we consider what Adams and Jefferson fervently believed America had to offer the rest of the world, we confront the ultimate irony. The lesson of history, Adams insisted, was to devise a political system to manage the conflict of different social classes. The lesson of history, Jefferson insisted, was to look to the American Revolution as the way out of oppression and despotism. Why would America need a political system designed to control the class systems of the Old World? Why would the Declaration of Independence be relevant to a foreign country that could hardly declare its natural, unalienable rights before it possessed them? Adams may have been wrong in seeing European realities taking root in America, but Jefferson was just as wrong in assuming that American ideals applied to a Europe that lacked the peculiar condition of a country that bypassed feudalism and had no ancien régime.

When Lafayette told Jefferson that he thought France would be wise in following Adams and setting up a bicameral legislature, the author of the Declaration shot back, "I am opposed to a democracy derived from love of liberty." Flabbergasted, the Frenchman could only wonder: Is not liberty the fount of all freedom? Not to Jefferson, for whom democracy meant far more than an institutional-based liberty that survives by means of checks and balances, what has come to be called liberal pluralism. Democracy must be direct, spontaneous, without the mediation of institutions, emanating straight from "the people," a category Adams saw as more rhetorical than real.

Whether looking to the popular masses, or to the balance of institutions, both Adams and Jefferson had little to offer the rest of a world struggling to be free. For the American Revolution was the only revolution in history where all classes fought together on the same side, a rare political phenomenon. Neither our second nor our third president sufficiently understood that independence, liberty, and equality resulted from exceptional American conditions unknown to the rest of the world. Since the time of Adams and Jefferson, America has tried to deal with a world raging with social conflict, only to be perplexed that revolutions, whether in France, Russia, Cuba, or Vietnam, fail to follow the American model. Neither president fully appreciated that America is about a consensus that is, given its rarity in history, next to a political miracle, and as such cannot be easily emulated or exported.

Adams, of course, believed that conflict emanated not from class systems but from human nature and its desire for recognition, irrational impulses that put people in competition with one another. Why, then, did President Adams not apply his own insights in social theory to what was going on in American politics? In *Discourses on Davila*, he made us aware that politics and social relations turn on representation, impression, images, and anything that shapes public opinion, and either enhances or destroys reputation. Ironically, it was Jefferson who was the first to recognize the power of the press in shaping opinion, the first to understand the possibilities of representation, even if it meant a little misrepresentation. As early as 1792, Hamilton sensed Jefferson's political skills in his *Catallus* essays, which were anonymously published in the press. But while Adams tried to govern, both Hamilton and Jefferson plotted against him. In the end, Jefferson had fewer quarrels with Adams than with Hamilton, with his preferences for establishing the banks, the judiciary, an army, and the authority of the nation-state. Yet Jefferson would not, because he could not, answer Adams when challenged to prove that the president intended to return the country to monarchy and aristocracy; he could hardly keep up his charge that Adams's doubts about the French Revolution should cause Americans to doubt their president when events in Paris unraveled to prove the wisdom of those doubts. However, with the Republicans as an opposition party and Hamilton as a fifth column in Adams's Federalist party, the charges leveled against Adams had only to be made, not validated. When politics is foul, anything is fair.

PRIDE BEFORE THE FALL
OF THE ADAMS PRESIDENCY

What, then, of the other impression that has redounded to the benefit of the Republicans: the view that their political outlook prevailed by virtue of winning elections while the Federalists receded into the twilight? Actually, by 1815, at the conclusion of the War of 1812, the world of Jeffersonianism was nowhere to be seen. The learned classics scholar Garry Wills effectively sums up the situation in his book on Jefferson's successor, James Madison. America won the war,

> but did Republican *policies* win? If opposition to centralization, federal power, and nationalism was crucial to their policies, then John Randolph had a point when he said that they won by losing their souls. Jefferson had opposed the Bank of the United States, public debt, a navy, a standing army, American manufacturing, federally funded improvement of the interior, the role of world power, military glory, an extensive foreign ministry, loose construction of the Constitution, and subordination of the states to the federal government. All those things were firmly back in place in the aftermath of the war.

While Wills sees the world of Jeffersonian republicanism as lost to the forces of history, he also sees the Federalists as having little claim to America for two reasons. First, out of the War of 1812 grew a passionate nationalism, while the New England Federalists, in contrast, had become the party of states' rights in opposing Jefferson's embargo, and thus they found themselves standing forth against the currents of history. Second, emerging out of this era of history, America embraced modernity as well as nationalism, whereas the Federalists had associated change in ways that clung to older social customs and religious values instead of looking forward to the new secular world of meritocracy and technology.

Neither the category of nationalism nor modernity applies to Adams since he embraced both. Unlike the New England Federalists, Adams in retirement opposed the secessionist sentiment at the Hartford Convention, and he supported Jefferson, Madison, and the War of 1812. As president, Adams did call for days of fasting, and he once quipped that those who no longer believe in God should "take opium." But his outlook was secular and modern, indeed even postmodern in his view that politics cannot depend upon philosophy, religion, or morality. Government is not a matter of "self-evident" truths but of institutional structures where power is checked by the psychology of suspicion. Adams's thoughts on the nature of power as an inexorable reality resembled those of Nietzsche and Niebuhr, and in her book *On Revolution*, Hannah Arendt admires Adams as one of the few eighteenth-century thinkers who saw that liberty, having been won in the Revolution, had to be institutionalized in the Constitution or it would have perished as a fiction without a foundation. "Why does power grow?" asked Adams. The modernists Nietzsche and Niebuhr, who likewise had doubts about the faculty of reason, raised the same question, seeing power as the sum of its effects, there to be called up by the will of the individual or controlled by the instruments of government. Adams said in 1788 what Lincoln said in 1838: The Constitution is necessary to protect people from their worst enemy—themselves.

What Adams dealt with in eighteenth-century thought is still debated today. In academic discourse, those who follow the philosopher John Dewey claim that our problem is not the people but the elites; adherents of Walter Lippmann claim that our problem is not the experts but the masses. Two centuries ago Adams stood between both points of view. Against Jefferson, Adams showed us that the problem was the many; against Hamilton, the few, all the more to be guarded against since the many would "emu-late" and defer to the rich. His *Defence* of the Constitution dealt with both classes.

The sad irony is that both the few and the many, Hamilton and Jefferson, joined forces to defeat him. In removing Adams from the seat of government, the election of 1800 freed the political mind of conscience and made America safe for sin. Ask not what you can do for your country but what you can do for yourself and do so in the name of whatever will sound right and proper. For is it not true, Adams wrote as a youth in "Self-Delusion," that we "flatter our-selves that our own intentions are pure, however sinister so ever they may be in fact," while we impute "vicious motives" to others and accept "word against evidence" in a world where those who deceive themselves are the ones "who may be interested in deceiv-ing us."

Responding to the accusations later made against him, the "vicious motives" of monarchism, Adams simply asked for evidence, not realizing what Henry Adams might have taught him: politics has no time for facts. Many of those who voted against him accepted "word against evidence" and thought they were ridding America of a monarchist, when they were actually deposing both a moralist and a modernist. Adams was a case of Niebuhr's "moral man in immoral society," a president who believed in honor and upheld ideals that, curiously enough, his own modernist theory of the "machinery of government" did not require. Convinced that human nature is inevitably egoistic and prone to sin, he believed that the president cannot count upon ideals as motives of action. Thus, the very virtues he asked of himself he doubted he would find in the people themselves.

With such skepticism, Adams criticized the precepts of classical republicanism, particularly those of Machiavelli, who was either deceiving himself or deceiving the citizens of Florence when he fed them "pious platitudes" about their patriotic ideals, just as Jefferson massaged the ego of the American people by praising their "genuine virtue." Rather than speak the truth and shame the devil, Machiavelli pleases the prince and flatters the people, while Jefferson extolls the "good sense" of the masses who enjoy "wisdom enough to manage the

concerns of society." Let there be popular self-government, and government itself need only govern least or not at all in a social environment of natural harmony.

It was the overriding importance of government that President
Adams tried to teach America. Yet Adams believed that if the institutions of government are well in place, its administration and
political management may be of no immediate, pressing urgency.
With that assumption, we come to the heart of the matter, the key
to Adams's limitations as a president, the possible explanation of
his failure.

While Adams convinced himself that Machiavelli had no idea
why republics consistently failed to survive, and that Jefferson had
no idea why government was necessary if the American republic
were to survive, perhaps the Italian philosopher could have taught
the American president how to succeed in office by engaging others
in the issues of the day. A prudent political leader, advised Machiavelli, "should always seek counsel" and be a "great inquisitor" and
"patient listener," avoiding the case of the "secretive nature" of the
prince who refuses to communicate with anyone.

Machiavelli may not have known why republics fail to survive,
but he could have taught Adams how to survive and perhaps even
succeed as a political leader. At times the sin of pride cursed the
Adams presidency. He often preferred to work alone, rarely sharing
his thoughts or seeking the input of others as he was making up his
mind. The controversial decision to send a mission to France backfired when it was sprung on the public. Adams was one of America's most solitary presidents, and the isolation of the mind, while
healthy for poetry or philosophy, is fatal in the sphere of politics.
Adams wrote his great books in the seclusion of his study, and the
lessons of the past lived in his writings; however, politics dwells in
the present, in bargains and distortions, maneuvers and manipula-
tions, and other strategies of exigency that had no appeal to a
thinker better at analyzing power than dealing with people. Adams
also bore grudges instead of trying to shed them. "A good citizen
out of love of country ought to ignore personal affronts," advised
Machiavelli. Adams's love of country proved incapable of helping
him overcome the affronts and attacks of Hamilton and Jefferson,

which hurt Abigail even more. The two worst things that can be said about President John Adams was that he behaved neither as a politician nor as a salesman, neither as one who would please his party by thinking only about the next election nor one who would stoop to peddling himself and his policies to the public.

Adams's keen sense of social psychology could easily have led him to manipulate opinion, court popularity, and play the opposition's game. He could have cast aspersion and suspicion on his rival, one who was rumored to have had a black teenage sexual playmate and known to have had his slaves whipped while claiming he knew that American farmers and plantation slave owners were "the chosen people of God." Adams was too much the moralist to do whatever is necessary to assure success, and too much the modernist to make easy moral judgments and to claim to know God's will.

Thus, a leader who valued government and hated politics lost to an opponent who hated government and was willing to stoop to politics even as he professed that he despised it and would choose not to go to heaven if it meant joining a political party. Jefferson saw himself slaying a phantom institution that no longer was; Adams saw himself trying to carry out a code of honor that no longer existed. The winner claimed he successfully saved us from monarchy; the loser tried to save us from mendacity. The politically involved Jefferson may have been sincere in his disavowal of politics and political parties. Even if he used the party and the press to take on the Adams presidency, his newly formed Republican Party would be, to use the expression of Richard Hofstadter, "a party to end parties," a national political effort in bringing the republic closer to his "quest for unanimity."

If unanimity were possible, politics would disappear and government wither away in a cloud of consensus. But Adams's sense of history led him to believe that there always was and always would be conflict, and the purpose of government was to control it. A Puritan in politics, Adams looked to the executive branch of government as the one office that could be held accountable, the place "where the buck stops," as the fiesty Harry Truman put it. Adams has been criticized as politically incorrect in his refusal to endorse democracy with heartfelt enthusiasm. Yet Adams did not count upon democracy to provide a moral conscience, and after 1800 politics functioned without one. Henceforth, there would be little relationship between theory and practice in electoral politics, little possibility that what a politician said while running for office would have any bearing on what he did once in office. With the increasing democratization of American political life, government left truth and morality behind to follow the path of power and expediency, rushing after public opinion and bowing to it, succumbing to what Tocqueville called parties of "consequence" rather than of "principle" and Emerson simply called a civic culture of "cunning," a politics of deception and clever image management—precisely what Adams anticipated in *Discourses on Davila*. But during Adams's four years in office, the buck did indeed stop, and for one, brief episode in American history the thought of truth shamed the tumult of politics.

Notes

WJA   *The Life and Works of John Adams*, ed. Charles Francis Adams (Boston, 1856), 10 vols.

DAJA   *The Diary and Autobiography of John Adams*, ed. L. H. Butterfield (Cambridge: Harvard University Press, 1961), 4 vols.

EDJA   *The Earliest Diary of John Adams*, ed. L. H. Butterfield (Cambridge: Harvard University Press, 1966).

JAD   John Adams, *Defence of the Constitutions of the United States of America* (1787–88; New York: DaCapo edition, 1971), 3 vols.

RWJA   *The Revolutionary Writings of John Adams*, ed. C. Bradley Thompson (Indianapolis: Liberty Fund, 2000).

AJL   *The Adams-Jefferson Letters*, ed. Lester J. Cappon (1959; New York: Clarion edition, 1971).

LJA   John Quincy Adams and Charles Francis Adams, *The Life of John Adams* (1871; New York: Haskell edition, 1968), 2 vols.

HAH   Henry Adams, *History of the United States During the Administrations of Thomas Jefferson and James Madison* (1889; New York: Library of America edition, 1986).

SOF   *The Spur of Fame: Dialogues of John Adams and Benjamin Rush* (1966; Indianapolis: Liberty Fund edition, 2001).

TJW   *Thomas Jefferson: Writings*, ed. Merrill D. Peterson (New York: Library of America, 1984).

PAH   *The Papers of Alexander Hamilton*, ed. Harold Syrett (New York: Columbia University Press, 1962), 22 vols.

INTRODUCTION: PLATO'S WISH

JA to TJ, Nov. 15, 1813, *AJL*, 397–402. JA to BR, Dec. 25, 1811, *SOF*, 217–20. JA, "On Private Revenge," *RWJA*, 14. Benjamin Constant, *De la Force du Gouvernement Actual* (1796; Paris: Flammarion edition, 1988), 77.

The best analysis of Adams as social theorist still remains Arthur O. Lovejoy, *Reflections on Human Nature* (Baltimore: Johns Hopkins University Press, 1961). Adams citing Shakespeare is in "Discourses on Davila," in *WJA*, VI, 262–70. G. W. F. Hegel, *The Phenomenology of Mind*, trans. J. B. Baillie (New York: Harper Torchback edition, 1967), 605. Curiously, Adams's critique of the French Revolution, in his *Discourses on Davila* (1790), presages that of the German philosopher Hegel, who would also see that the Revolution's theory of freedom "effaces and annuls" all differences. See Sidney Hook, "Hegel and the Perspective of Liberalism," in *Pragmatism and the Tragic Sense of Life* (New York: Basic, 1974), 115–36. TJ to William Short, Jan. 3, 1794, *TJW*, 1003–06; Adams on law in *WJA*, IV, 408; *The Lincoln-Douglas Debates of 1858*, ed. Robert W. Johannsen (New York: Oxford, 1965), 219–37, 277–84. Adams on nobles tyrannizing, in *JAD*, II, 46; on Aristotle, *JAD*, II, 165–66; on Plato, *JAD*, I, 188–211; JA to TJ, July 16, 1814, *AJL*, 434–39. Madison on Plato, *Federalist*, no. 49, and absence of enlightened statesmen, no. 10. JA to TJ, Oct. 9, 1787, *AJL*, 202–03. Jefferson on "ploughman," TJ to Peter Carr, Aug. 10, 1787, *TJW*, 900–04, on "chosen people of God" in "Notes on Virginia" in *TJW*, 290–91. Henry Adams to Elizabeth Cameron, Mar. 3, 1901, *The Letters of Henry Adams*, ed. J. C. Levinson et al., 6 vols. (Cambridge: Harvard University Press, 1982), V, 212. Adams on Washington and Franklin in *WJA*, IX, 636. Franklin on Adams in Edmund S. Morgan, *Benjamin Franklin* (New Haven: Yale University Press, 2002), 294. Jefferson on dependency in *TJW*, 290–91. Adams on democracy as Lovelace, in a letter to William Cunningham, Esq., quoted in Gilbert Chirard, *Honest John Adams* (1933; Boston: Little, Brown edition, 1964), 321. Adams on dinner and girl, JA to John Taylor, Apr. 15, 1814, in *The Political Writings of John Adams*, ed. George A. Peek Jr. (Indianapolis: Bobbs-Merrill, 1954), 206. No doubt John Adams would disagree with the sketch I attempted of his physical features, as he did of attempts by contemporaries. "I have no Miniature," he responded to a question, "and have been too much abused by Painters ever to sit to any one again." "My head has been so long the sport of painters, as my heart has been of libellers," he wrote in 1813. A few years later he was more irksome. "The age of sculpture and painting have not yet arrived in this country and I hope it will not arrive very soon. Arists have done what they pleased with my face and eyes, head and shoulders, stature and figure and they have made of them monsters as fit for exhibition as Harlequin or Punch." Quoted in Andrew Oliver, *Portraits of John and Abigail Adams* (Cambridge: Harvard University Press, 1967), 1–3.

1: FROM "SENSELESS TURPITUDE" TO STATELY DUTY

EDJA, 3–56; *WJA*, I–II; Chinard, 3–43; Edith Gelles, *Portia: The World of Abigail Adams* (Bloomington: Indiana University Press, 1992); Page Smith, *John Adams*, 2 vols. (New York: Doubleday, 1962), I, 57–71; David McCullough,

John Adams (New York: Simon & Schuster, 2001), 17–110, 125–332; *The Book of Abigail and John: Selected Letters of the Adams Family, 1762–1784*, eds. L. H. Butterfield, Marc Friedlaender, and Mary-Jo Kline (Cambridge: Harvard University Press, 1975), 327–82; Adams's early political writings are in *RWJA*. Adams's ethnic remarks quoted in Patricia Bradley (who drew upon the hearings on the Boston Massacre), *Slavery, Propaganda, and the American Revolution* (Jackson: University of Mississippi Press, 1998), 61–62; on Adams's reflections on his experience with European diplomacy, *DAJA*, II; on Adams's irritableness and the diplomatic nuances of distrust, James H. Hutson, "The American Negotiators: The Diplomacy of Jealousy," in *Peace and the Peacemakers: The Treaty of 1783*, eds. Ronald Hoffman and Peter J. Albert (Charlottesville: University Press of Virginia, 1986), 52–69.

2: "THE MOST INSIGNIFICANT OFFICE THAT EVER MAN CONTRIVED"

On the London years and the vice presidency, Smith, II, 642–893; McCullough, 333–465; on Adams's Federalist antagonist, Forrest McDonald, *Alexander Hamilton: A Biography* (New York: Norton, 1982); Richard Brookheiser, *Alexander Hamilton: American* (New York: Simon & Schuster, 1999); the description of Maclay as "the original Jeffersonian" is in Charles A. Beard, "Introduction," *The Journals of William Maclay* (New York: Boni, 1927) v. On the tensions between Adams and Jefferson, Joseph J. Ellis, *Passionate Sage: The Character and Legacy of John Adams* (New York: Norton, 1994); on further research and reflections on Jefferson moving covertly to do political damage to Adams, Ellis, *Founding Brothers: The Revolutionary Generation* (New York: Knopf, 2000). Jefferson's denials that he is interested in politics and has any affinity toward political parties, and his conviction, or suspicion, that there is nothing to stop the presidency as an institution from perpetuating itself, are in various letters in *TJW*, 941–42, 1033–39, 1041–44, 1048–54, 1218–22. For his description of Adams as "favorable to monarchy" as evidenced in "Davila," *TJW*, 671–72. His conviction on tolerating differences, Daniel J. Boorstin, *The Lost World of Thomas Jefferson* (Boston: Beacon, 1948); James Callender, Jefferson's hired hack, sought to convince Hamilton that Adams had attempted to use his position as vice president to turn the Senate into the aristocratic branch of government. Adams, of course, did see the Senate serving somewhat that function since he assumed superior people would be elected to it, but he so envisioned the structure of government that the Senate would be kept under close surveillance and separate from the House whose common members would otherwise be easily manipulated. Tom Callender, Esq., *Letters to Alexander Hamilton: King of the Feds* (New York: Reynolds, 1802). Adams on the temptation to accusation is in *WJA*, VI, 378. A valuable study of the two antagonists is Merrill D. Peterson, *Adams and Jefferson: A*

Revolutionary Dialogue (New York: Oxford, 1975). This author is much tougher on Jefferson than the genteel treatment offered by Professor Peterson. The difference may be geograpical; he teaches in Virginia, I in New York; in one state property rules, as Jefferson hoped; in the other money rules, as Adams predicted.

3: THE PRESCIENCE OF THE POLITICAL MIND

WJA, II, 419–23; Samuel Eliot Morison, *The Conservative American Revolution* (Washington, D.C.: Society of the Cincinnati, 1976), 6–7; Gabrielle Bonnot de Mably, *Observations sur le gouvernement et loix Etats-Unis d'Amerique* (1784), *Oeuvres completes* (London, 1789), vol. 8, 301–408; on the French response to America's moving toward the idea of a "mixed government," Denis LaCorne, *L'invention de la republique: Le modele Americain* (Paris: Hachette, 1991); also Rene Remond, *Les Etats-Unis Devant L'Opinion Francaise* (Paris: Armand Colin, 1962); all quotations from Adams's political philosophy from *JAD*, I, II, and *WJA*, IV; on Adams's insisting America has no use for monarchy, *JAD*, III, 371–72; on Adams's critique of the classical concept of virtue, John Patrick Diggins, *The Lost Soul of American Politics: Virtue, Self-Interest, and the Foundations of Liberalism* (New York: Basic, 1984); on Adams's political writings, C. Bradley Thompson, *John Adams and the Spirit of Liberty* (Lawrence: University of Kansas Press, 1998); of the historians' criticisms, Gordon S. Wood, *The Creation of the American Republic* (Chapel Hill: University of North Carolina Press, 1969), 586–89; Sean Wilentz, "America Made Easy: McCullough, Adams, and the Decline of Popular History," *New Republic* (July 2, 2001), 35–40; a study that shows how Adams can be traced from David Hume and Adam Smith to Thorstein Veblen may be found in Arthur O. Lovejoy, *Reflections on Human Nature* (Baltimore: Johns Hopkins University Press, 1961). Jefferson quoted from *TJW*, 290–91; Reinhold Niebuhr, *The Nature and Destiny of Man*, vol. I, *Human Nature* (New York: Scribners, 1941), 91. Adams's thoughts are similar to those of Niebuhr and Nietzsche in exposing man's capacity for self-deception and the tendency to rationalize interest-driven behavior in the name of high ideals. On Adams and Rousseau, Zoltan Haraszti, *John Adams and the Prophets of Progress* (New York: Grosset & Dunlap, 1964); on Rousseau, Isaiah Berlin, *Freedom and Its Betrayal: Six Enemies of Human Liberty* (London: Chatto & Windus, 2002), 27–49; for an appreciation of Adams by a contemporary French scholar and magistrate, Jean-Paul Goffinon, *Aux Origines de la Revolution Americaine: John Adams: La Passion de la Distinction* (Bruxelles: University de Bruxelles, 1996); for Adams and French political philosophers, Joyce Appleby, "John Adams and the New Republican Synthesis," in *Liberalism and Republicanism in the Historical Imagination* (Cambridge: Harvard University Press, 1992), 188–209; John Patrick Diggins, "John Adams and the French Critics of the American Constitution," in *To Form a More Perfect Union: The Critical Ideas of the*

Constitution, eds. Herman Belz, Ronald Hoffmann, Peter J. Albert (Char-
lottesville: University of Virginia, 1992), 104–33; Edward Handler, *America
and Europe in the Political Thought of John Adams* (Cambridge: Harvard
University Press, 1964); Sieyès on the nation quoted in Keith Michael
Baker, "Souverainete," in Francois Furet and Mona Ozouf, *Dictionnaire Critique de la Revolution Francaise: Idées* (Paris: Flammarion, 1992), 483–505.
Adams's daughter on her father's "disgusted at the match" in *Journal and
Correspondence of Miss Adams* (New York: Wiley and Putnam, 1841),
21–47; Jefferson on the French Revolution, TJ to William Short, Jan. 2,
1793, *TJW,* 1003–06; see also Conor Cruise O'Brien, *The Long Affair:
Thomas Jefferson and the French Revolution, 1785–1800* (Chicago: University of Chicago Press, 1996); Paine's letter to Washington in *Thomas Paine:
Representative Selections,* ed. Harry Hayden Clark (New York: Hill & Wang,
1944), 392–93.

4: THE HALO OF WASHINGTON, THE SHADOW OF JEFFERSON

Aratus on Adams's monarchism, *TJW,* 670–72; Marco Sioli, "Citizen Genet
and the Political Struggle in the Early American Republic," *Revue Francaise
d'Etudes Americaines,* 64 (1995), 259–67. Gerald A. Combs, *The Jay Treaty:
Political Battleground of the Founding Fathers* (Berkeley: University of California Press, 1970); Smith, 878–93; McCullough, 389–455. Thomas
Slaughter, *The Whiskey Rebellion: Frontier Epilogue to the American Revolution* (New York: Oxford University Press, 1986); Adams on Hamilton as
"the bastard brat," JA to BR, Jan. 25, 1806, *SOF,* 49–51; on the distrusting
Adams becoming even more distrustful about the possibility of honesty in
human relations, Joanne B. Freeman "The Presidential Election of 1796," in
John Adams and the Founding of the Republic, ed. Richard Alan Ryerson
(Boston: Massachusetts Historical Society, 2001), 142–70. Madison's
remarks on Adams are in Richard K. Matthews, *If Men Were Angels: James
Madison and the Heartless Empire of Reason* (Lawrence: University of
Kansas, 1995), 6–7; for Adams's cabinet, Stanley Elkins and Eric McKit-
rick, *The Age of Federalism: The Early American Republic, 1788–1800* (New
York: Oxford, 1993), 529–79; *LJA,* II, 214–19, 307–22; on the "pinched"
president and Abigail and the black servant and student, Smith, 914–26.

5: THE FRENCH: FOE OR FRIEND?

Louis C. Kleber, "The XYX Affair," *History Today,* 23 (1973), 715–23;
William Stinchcombe, "The Diplomacy of the XYZ Affair," *William and
Mary Quarterly,* 34 (1977), 590–617; Thomas M. Ray, "Not One Cent for
Tribute: The Public Addresses and American Popular Reaction to the XYZ
Affair, 1798–1799," *Journal of the Early American Republic,* 3 (1983),
389–412; *LJA,* 227–52; Smith, 952–65; Elkins and McKitrick, 528–78; JA
to TJ, Aug. 4, 1785, *AJL,* 48–49; *WJA,* IV, 354; I. Bernard Cohen, *Science*

and the Founding Fathers (New York: Norton, 1995); message to Congress, May 16, 1797, in *WJA*, IX, 111–19; Michel Missoffe, *Le Coeur Secret de Talleyrand* (Paris: Librarie Academie, 1956), 101–19; Pieter Geyl, "The French Historians and Talleyrand," in *Debates with Historians* (New York: Meredian, 1958). Jefferson on the Portuguese ambassador quoted in Albert Jay Nock, *Mr. Jefferson* (Tampa: Halberg, 1983), 136; on Abigail's wrath toward journalists, Edith Gelles, "'Splendid Misery': Abigail Adams as First Lady," in Ryerson, 186–234.

6: WAR MEASURES, FREE SPEECH, STATES' RIGHTS

Adams's "no such thing" in Elkins and McKitrick, 590; various views of historians surveyed in Richard D. Brown, "The Disenchantment of a Radical Whig: John Adams Reckons with Free Speech," in Ryerson, 171–85; descriptions of Priestley and Callender in William Channing, *History of the United States*, 10 vols. (New York: Macmillan, 1917), IV, 220. *La France & L'Irlande Pendant la Revolution: D'apres les documents inedits des archieves de France et d'Irlande*, ed. E. Guillon (Paris: Armand Colin, 1888), 466–77; Maurice J. Bric, "The Irish and the Evolution of the 'New Politics' in America," *Irish Studies*, 4 (1985), 143–67. Abigail on Lyon, in Smith, 949–50; on journalists, Gelles, 186–234; for the historians on the Alien and Sedition Acts, Elkins and McKitrick, 694–701; McCullough, 504–05, 521, 566; Smith, 975–78. The critical view, where Gallatin is quoted, is Andrew Lenneer, "Separate Spheres: Republican Constitutionalism in the Federalist Era," *The American Journal of Legal History*, 41 (1997), 251–81; Peter S. Onuf and Leonard J. Sadosky, *Jeffersonian America* (Oxford: Blackwell, 2002), 198–99; Richard Rosenfeld, "The Adams Tyranny," *Harper's*, 303 (Sept. 2001), 82–86; on Gerry's letters to Adams, Eugene Kramer, "Some New Light on the XYZ Affair: Elbridge Gerry's Reasons for Opposing War with France," *New England Quarterly*, 29 (1956), 509–13; Abigail's description of Gerry in Smith, 968; TJ to Abigail Adams, July 22, 1804, *AJL*, 274–76; Adams on government, *WJA*, IV, 402–03; Richard Samuelson, "John Adams and the Republic of Laws" (forthcoming); Henry quoted in Channing, 230–31.

7: THE AMERICAN LANDSCAPE

Records of the Federal Convention of 1787, 4 vols., ed. Max Farand (New Haven: Yale University Press, 1966), I, 66, 83, 132. The descriptions and quotations about conditions in America from *HAH*, I, 5–53; Jefferson on science staying independent of public service quoted in Morgan, *Franklin*, 27. Discussion of the Fries's Rebellion and prosecution and Adams's pardoning all from "Special Issue: The Fries Rebellion," ed. Simon Newman, *Pennsylvania History*, 67 (Winter 2000); *PAH*, XXIV, 444–53; William Lewis to Alexander Hamilton, Oct. 11, 1800, *PAH*, XXV, 151–57. JA to TJ, June 30,

1813, *AJL*, 346–48; on tax revolts in European history, Le Roy Ladurie, *Carnival in Romans*, trans. Mary Feeney (New York: Braziller, 1980), xv, 361–63. Hamilton to McHenry, Mar. 8, 1799, *PAH*, XXII, 552–53.

8: WAR AND PEACE

The discussion of Adams at the capital and Quincy and Abigail's illness and the dissolution of son Charles and other matters all from Smith, 1036–82; McCullough, 508–31. Jefferson's horror on Adams's recognizing Toussaint-Louverture in McCullough, 521; also Michael Zuckerman, "The Power of Blackness: Thomas Jefferson and the Revolution in Saint-Domingue," in *Almost Chosen People: Oblique Biographies in the American Grain* (Berkeley: University of California Press, 1993), Conor Cruise O'Brien, 280–93; C. L. R. James, *The Black Jacobins* (1938; New York: Vintage edition, 1962); Jefferson to Lafayette in Saint-Beuve, *Portraits Litteraires* (Paris: Laffont, 1993), 480; on slavery, JA to Robert J. Evans, June 8, 1819, in *The American Enlightenment*, ed. Adriene Koch (New York: Brazillier, 1965), 230–31. Pickering quoted in Elkins and McKitrick, 662; Steven G. Kurtz, "President Adams Chooses Peace," in *The Federalists: Creators and Critics of the Union, 1780–1801*, ed. Steven G. Kurtz (New York: Wiley, 1972), 185–97; McDonald, *Hamilton*, 347; Channing, 208; JA to BR, June 20, 1808, *SOF*, 119–21; *LJA*, II, 173, 179; JA to James McHenry, Oct. 22, 1798, *WJA*, VIII, 612–14; "Conversation with Arthur Fenner," June 25–26, 1800, *PAH*, XXIV, 595–97; "A Letter from Alexander Hamilton, Concerning the Public Conduct of John Adams, Esq, President of the United States," *PAH*, XXV, 169–234; Gore Vidal, *Burr* (New York: Random House, 1973), 2; John Bartlow Martin, *Adlai Stevenson of Illinois* (Garden City, N.Y.: Doubleday, 1976), 759; "Be not concerned," Smith, 1055; JA to BR, June 20, 1808, *SOF*, 119–21; Arthur Schlesinger Jr., *The Cycles of American History* (Boston: Houghton Mifflin, 1986); TJ to Abigail Adams, *AJL*, July 22, 1804, 274–76; McCullough, 583–85; Ellis, *Founding Brothers*, 206–27; response to Mercy Otis Warren, McCullough, 595; TJ to JA, Feb. 15, 1825; JA to TJ, Feb. 25, 1825, *AJL*, 608–10.

CONCLUSION: THE MORALIST IN POLITICS

JAD, II, 44; TJ to John Taylor, June 4, 1798, *TJW*, 1048–51; Richard Samuelson, "What Adams Saw Over Jefferson's Wall," *Commentary*, 104 (Aug. 1997), 52–54; the *Gazette* quoted in Andrew W. Robertson, "'Look on this Picture . . . And on This!' Nationalism, Localism, and Partisan Images of Otherness in the United States, 1787–1820," *American Historical Review*, 106 (Oct. 2001), 1263–80; Joanne B. Freeman, *Affairs of Honor: National Politics in the New Republic* (New Haven: Yale University Press, 2001); John Howe Jr., "Republican Thought and Political Violence of the 1790s," *American Quarterly*, 19 (Summer 1987), 146–65; JA to TJ, July 13,

1813, Dec. 21, 1819, *AJL*, 353–56, 550–51. Bertrand Russell, *Power* (New York: Unwin Books, 1962); Edmund Burke, *Reflections on the Revolution in France*, ed. William Todd (New York: Rhinehart, 1959), 238–39; Hamilton's *Catallus* is Sept. 29, 1792, in *PAH*, XII, 498–506; Garry Wills, *James Madison* (New York: Times Books, 2002), 151; JA, "Self-Delusion," *RWJA*, 7–12; Niccolò Machiavelli, *The Discourses*, trans. Leslie J. Walker, S.J., ed. Bernard Crick (New York: Penguin, 1983), 523; "The Prince," in *The Portable Machiavelli*, eds. Peter Bondanella and Mark Musa (New York: Viking, 1979), 156. Richard Hofstadter, *The Idea of a Party System: The Rise of Legitimate Opposition in the United States, 1780–1840* (Berkeley: University of California Press, 1969), 151.

Milestones

1735   Born in Braintree (later Quincy), Massachusetts.
1755   Graduates from Harvard College.
1758   Admitted to the Boston Bar.
1764   Marries Abigail Smith.
1765   Writes *Dissertation on the Canon and Feudal Law.*
1770   Boston Massacre; defends Captain Preston.
1775   Chosen to the Continental Congress.
      Writes "Novanglus."
1776   Writes *Thoughts on Government* in reply to Thomas Paine's *Common Sense.*
      Thomas Jefferson writes the Declaration of Independence.
1777   Elected commissioner to France.
1780   Appointed minister to Holland.
1783   Peace treaty with England.
1784   Rejoins Abigail and their daughter in London; returns to Paris
1785   Settles in at Grosvenor Square, London; envoy to the Court of St. James.
1786   Daughter marries Colonel William Smith.
      Begins writing *Defence of the Constitutions.*
1786–87   Shays's Rebellion in Massachusetts.
      First volume of *Defence* published in New York and Philadelphia (two subsequent volumes published in 1788).
1788   The Adamses return to Massachusetts.
      Elected vice president.
1790   *Discourses on Davila* published.
      Thomas Jefferson blurbs Thomas Paine's *The Rights of Man.*
      The newspaper wars begin in Philadelphia.
1792   Reelected vice president.
1794   The Whiskey Rebellion.
1794   Washington appoints John Quincy Adams minister to the Hague.

1796   Elected president.
1797–98   XYZ Affair.
1798   Alien and Sedition Acts.
1799   The Fries's Rebellion.
        Napoleon comes to power in France.
1800   Loses election to Jefferson.
        Son Charles dies.
1801   Peace settlement with France.
        Returns to Quincy.
1803   Louisiana Purchase.
1808   Madison elected president.
1812   United States declares war on England.
1813   Begins correspondence with Jefferson.
1814   Daughter Nabby dies; responds to John Taylor's *An Inquiry*.
1815   Peace treaty with England.
1816   James Monroe elected president.
1818   Abigail Adams dies.
1823   John Quincy Adams outlines the Monroe Doctrine.
1824   John Quincy Adams elected president.
1826   Dies.

Acknowledgments

My appreciation to Elizabeth Harlan for her helpful comments, Richard Samuleson for saving me from errors of fact and interpretation, and to Jean-Paul Goffinon for his valuable conversations on the subject.

The book was written in Paris in a residence close to the corner where the rues Condorcet and Turgot meet. Once admiring friends of John Adams, Jean Antoine Nicholas de Condorcet and Baron Anne-Robert Turgot became severe critics of America's new Federal Constitution of 1788. The critisisms prompted Adams to write a three-volume defense of America's state and national constitutions and another text, published in 1790 just before he became vice president, a commentary on some Parisian *philosophes* and their all-too-earnest beliefs in the Enlightenment.

These texts later provided the grounds for accusing the president of the United States of being a secret monarchist. The Adams who had once eloquently articulated the case for the American Revolution also refused to support the French Revolution. Ironically, Adams's antagonists opposed his presidency in defense of state sovereignty; yet they supported a revolution abroad that represented the very centralization of national authority that they abhorred at home. Untroubled by inconsistency, they saw lurking in the presidency a clear and present danger: a counterrevolutionary in the grip of the "glare of royalty."

In the 1790s, John Adams reflected on the events in France; in the 1980s, Paul Berman on the events in Nicarauga. Both faced the wrath of some of their own friends for telling us that a revolution without representation is destined to devour itself. Truth dared to speak before its time.

Index

ABOUT THE AUTHOR

John Patrick Diggins is a distinguished professor of history at the Graduate Center of the City University of New York. He is the author of numerous books, including *On Hallowed Ground* and *The Proud Decades*. He lives in New York City.